Cover: The Metropolitan Museum
(edited)

Qurrat Ayun Al-Akhiar, Bulaq Press, 1299 Hijri

This issue is supported in part by:

NORTHWESTERN
UNIVERSITY
IN QATAR

ARABLIT QUARTERLY

VOLUME 4, ISSUE 2
Summer 2021

Guest Editor: Nour Kamel

Editor-in-chief: M Lynx Qualey
Art Director: Hassân Al Mohtasib
Managing Editor: Nashwa Gowanlock
Contributing Editors:
Sawad Hussain, Olivia Snaije,
Nariman Youssef, Lucie Taylor,
Joel Mitchell, Ranya Abdel Rahman
Editorial Assistant:
Leonie Rau
Research Consultant:
Amanda Hannoosh Steinberg

A production of www.arablit.org
Opinions, submissions, advertising:
info@arablit.org
© All rights reserved

ط / ب / خ

Ta' – Ba' – Kha'

◆ **INTRODUCTION**

4   by Nour Kamel

◆ **FEATURES**

18   **Teita's Bitter Orange Jam**
     By Salma Serry

40   **Making Mahshi**
     By Sohila Khaled

50   **'It Was to Her a Ritual'**
     By Zaina Ujayli

60   **Of Figs & Grapes**
     By Leonie Rau

64   **On Fiction's Uneaten Meals**
     Donia Kamal, interviewed by Asmaa Abdallah

88   **Mind Your Table Manners**
     By Badr al-Din al-Ghazzi
     translated by Hacı Osman Gündüz (Ozzy)

104 **The Waiting in Waraq Enab**
     By Yasmine Shamma

126 **Read & Eat: Sandwiches Before the Earl**
     By Nawal Nasrallah

◆ **WORKSHOP**

70   **The Taste of Letters**
     By Nour Kamel

72   **How I Cook Love in Three Steps**
     By Eman Abdelhamid Kamal
     translated by Mariam Boctor

76   **From Farm to Table**
     By Moza Almatrooshi

78   **The Loaf of Bread We Broke Together**
     By Samaa Elturkey
     translated by Mariam Boctor

82   **The Meeting Space**
     By Rania Hilal
     translated by Elissa Dallimore

86   **Beyond A Herring Recipe**
     By Amira Mousa
     translated by Mahitab Mahmoud

◆ **SHORT FICTION**

120 **Chocolate Cake**
     By Mohamed Khalfouf
     translated by Mbarek Sryfi

124 **Rice Pudding for Two**
     By Rehab Bassam
     translated by Fatima El-Kalay

◆ **POETRY**

36   **My Mother's Kitchen**
38   **A Kitchen of My Own**
     By Rym Jalil
     translated by Mariam Boctor

Of Figs & Grapes
PAGE 60

Introduction

"**It is said that there are three things that are nerve-racking: a lamp that does not give light, a slow messenger, and waiting at a table for a guest running late.**" Badr al-Din al-Ghazzi, translated by Hacı Osman Gündüz (Ozzy)

I am usually the guest running late. Often, I offer my apologies for doing so with something sweet I've baked or bought. None of my friends have sworn off me yet, and I continue to receive invitations to dinner despite being always, without fail, infamously tardy. So I offer this as a remedy if, like me, you lose track of time more often than not.

By Nour Kamel

I'm late in writing this introduction, skimming through the pages of this issue for the millionth time because I'm trying to get all the right words down to describe it. I wanted this issue to platform writers I've worked with, writers I love, and writers whose words all come together to talk about something integral to our lives: food. A cornerstone of identity-making, especially in the SWANA region and for many Arabic speakers, food is the lifeblood of family and community. It is a unifier, a cultural symbol, how we remember our history and traditions, and above all a glorious, satiating pastime.

This is not a rose-colored reading of food, or kitchens, or eating—our relationship to all this is complex. In these pages, there is proof. There are family dynamics tempered by the issue of space(s) in poetry by Rym Jalil, social and personal dynamics that bleed into our food in Amira Mousa's insistence on not writing about food, and an attempt at a chocolate cake that helps Mohamed Khalfouf understand his mother's labor and love of cooking.

I was excited for the opportunity to guest edit an issue all about food: the act of cooking it, the spaces it inhabits in all of our lives, its histories, its meanings, and its intricacies. This issue is as playful as it is longingly, desperately serious—often, I have found, these two things bittersweetly coexist. Sohila Khaled's illustrated recipe for mahshi flows joyfully across the page, while in her essay, "The Waiting in Waraq Enab," Yasmine Shamma struggles to make this same meal, which, for her, is imbued with loss and longing.

Palestine stands central in my heart always and through these pages, even in its absence. The texts here teem with the ramifications of access and displacement, and how it affects our traditions intrinsically linked to food and our (literal and cultural) survival. Not only is food an inevitability of our survival, it is an inevitable relationship we forge for a lifetime—one that endures a process of loss, or which we adapt out of necessity, as Zaina Ujayli poignantly writes about while rifling through the archive of early-20th-century Syrian American women writers. On both the individual and communal level, the complexity of food wants to be unpacked, and the voices in these pages attempt to do so across different continents, eras, and ongoing struggles.

A plethora of essays, most of them personal, fill these pages. This issue features translations of five Arabic texts which I had the honor of helping their writers build over two months during the "Taste of Letters" workshop. My driving intention as guest editor for this issue was to finally have them not only translated into English, but reach a wider audience. These texts speak to each other, and to my surprise but not shock, they resonated with the rest of the majority submission-based pieces.

Whether referring to blood or chosen families, most of these texts are written with community, ancestry, and kinship as central themes, which bind and formulate our relationships to each other and to our food. They shape and recur in these pieces, from recipes handed down by grandmothers—as Salma Serry walks us beautifully through the making of mirabbet lareng and the fascinating, complex history of the woman from whom she inherited it—to the moments we choose (or choose not) to share the intimate act of cooking and devouring—as Rehab Bassam depicts in a joyful, solitary, Fairouz-filled making of roz bil laban.

My hope for this issue was for it to showcase the diversity with which contemporary Arabic writers are addressing food, cooking, and the act of care—be it for themselves or others. The act of eating is one we do to sustain, even delight (or dala3) ourselves, and when we cook for others it is an extension of us: our life-force, our energy, our caring for others. There is no more intimate act that hinges on a lack of immediate reciprocity: to feed and sate others. And even though I am always late when others offer to feed me, I make sure that this act of care is returned in kind—with a little bit of sweetness added.

Previous spread:
Sfax, Tunisia
Above: Morocco
Right: Palestine
© Pixabay, Pexels,
Library of Congress,
Unsplash

Left: Jordan
Below: Algeria
Library of Congress

Essay

Teita's Bitter Orange Jam

Home Economics, Umm Kulthum, & Gamal Abdel Nasser

By **Salma Serry**

Photography: Salma Serry and Omar Baderkhan

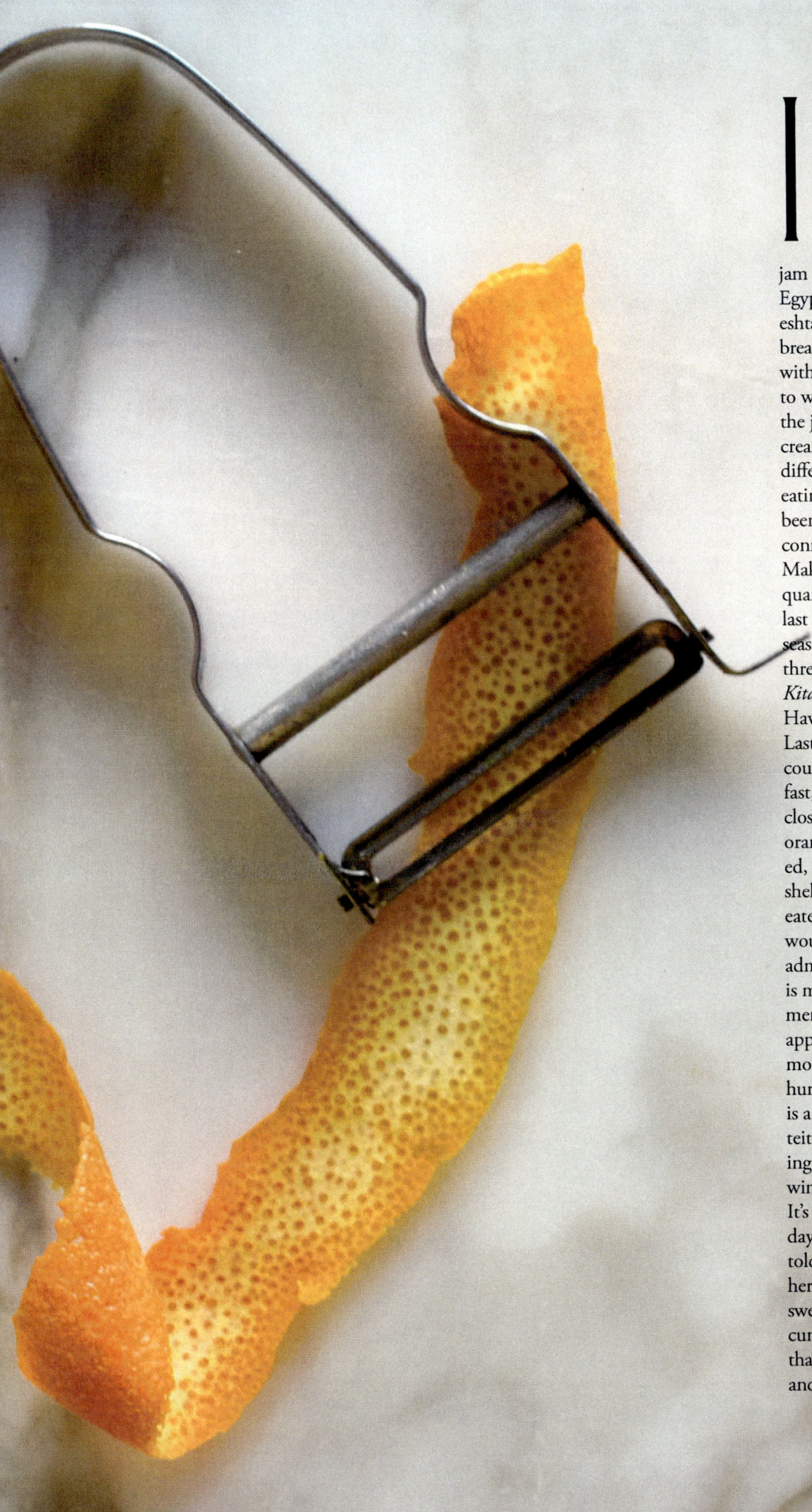

It's a bright and blistering morning in the middle of July here in Cairo. At first I think I really don't need to be having breakfast outside on the balcony today. But I convince myself that if I have a little of the bitter orange jam (known as mirabbet lareng in Egypt), swirled in some fresh cold eshta, or clotted cream, with baladi bread, then I'll be hitting three birds with one stone. First, I might be able to withstand some of the heat with the jam's citrus freshness and the cold cream. Second, there is something different about the experience of eating food made with a recipe that's been around for almost 90 years, a connection beyond sense and taste. Making the jam was a little Covid-19 quarantine experiment I embarked on last winter, when the oranges were in season, and after I was handed down three of my grandmother's cookbooks: *Kitab al-Ta'lim al-Manzeli*, Hadaya Hawaa's Jams, and *Usul al-Tahy*. Lastly and most usefully, by taking a couple of tablespoons for this breakfast, I would slowly but surely come closer to finishing the 15 jars of bitter orange jam the experiment had yielded, and which now sat on two cold shelves in the fridge, waiting to be eaten. I kept asking my friends if they would like a couple of jars, but they admitted they were not fans. Neither is my husband. So, to my disappointment, I remained the sole eater and appreciator of these 15 jars for six months. I admit, my jam ego was hurt. I understand that not everyone is a fan and not everyone shares my teita's history but, really, there is nothing like this perfect preservation of winter's nature to welcome summer. It's a taste from my grandmother's days, and a reminder of the stories she told me when I was a little girl. It is her life packed in a jar: a mélange of sweet aspirations, bitter financial circumstances, and sticky political events that shaped her relationship to food, and everything that she was.

The Home Economics Movement

At 10 years old, following her mother's premature death, Widad (my teita) went to live with her maternal aunt Aisha, who was a graduate of Madrasat al-Thaqafa al-Nasawiyyah. Loosely, this translates as "The School of Women's Culture." With her six girl cousins and a building full of second cousins around her age, the years Widad spent there would make plenty of happy memories. Like the other girls in the family, she went to a girls-only school that laid special importance on domestic science. Classes in laundry and ironing, sewing and embroidery, as well as cooking and baking were a standard in girls' schools of the time. She particularly enjoyed the cooking classes, where she and her classmates—all dressed in navy blue skirts and white shirts, with ribbons in their braided hair—would gather around a table and watch their teacher create all sorts of dishes. There was tomato sauce, baton sale, puddings, dolmas, and, of course, bitter orange jam. She would neatly write the recipe down based on her observations and then give her notebook to the teacher for grading. Her now-fragile and stained notebook, with the recipe for bitter orange jam dated 1950 and marked with her teacher's red ink check, sits today in my library in a transparent sleeve, along with newspaper and magazine clippings of other recipes.

Her own grandmother, Neina Zainab, who lived in the same building, was a proud owner of a large clay oven, which sat on the rooftop and which she would use for daily lunch casseroles as well as festive baking. Every week before the two Eid holidays, all the women of the building, as well as family and friends, would gather with their children on the roof and sit on kilim rugs, filling trays of traditional kahk stuffed with dates, walnuts, pistachios, and honey paste for themselves, their neighbors, and the community. Taking advantage of access to the rooftop oven, Widad would make her favorite pastafrolla pie (a Greek jam pie) with her bitter orange jam, using her textbook *Kitab al-Ta'lim al-Manzeli* by Fatma Fahmi. She would put the pie in to be baked with the rest of the Eid cookies.

Fahmi's book was her textbook in school. It is one of the earliest cookbooks to be taught in Egyptian schools, following Mounira Francis's *al-Tabkh al-Manzeli* (1914) and Jamila al-Alayli's *Sa'adat al-Mar'aah* (1925). The book is rich in references to European and British recipes, such as rock biscuits, puddings, Victoria sponge cake, and tea cakes—all of which are often paired with jams. It draws a vivid picture of the prevalence of a knowledge base, economic system, and culture modelled after British ideals and values, during a time when Egypt was under British occupation. In fact, Fahmi was one of hundreds of women to receive state-funded scholarships to study home economics in England. In her case, as she states in the book, she was a graduate of the Training College of Domestic Subjects, Berridge House, Hampstead, in London, which was established in 1909 by the National Society for Promoting Religious Education. The college boasted a state-of-the-art science laboratory and was the first domestic science college in Britain to appoint a lecturer with a science degree. ▪

My grandparents, Samira and Abdulaziz Attia in Cairo, 1950s

1 Rayner-Canham and Rayner-Canham, 2011. *The Rise and Fall of Domestic Chemistry In Higher Education In England During The Early 20th Century.*

2 *Fahmi, 1930. Kitab al-Ta'lim al-Manzeli. Wizaret al-Maarif al-Umumiyyah. Cairo.*

Considered by some an antidote to the social imbalances that resulted from early capitalism and industrialization, home economics was regarded as one of the strategies undertaken to fix the ailments of society by economizing and organizing the way households were managed. In the book's introduction, Fahmi describes how European nations realized the importance of the art of home economics and its role in fixing (*eslah*) the "environments" and straightening up (*taqweem*) the family, "no matter how humble its income." **2** This domain's whole premise and literal name, "home economics," relies on the principles of resource management, efficient production, and waste reduction, in an effort to support and manage (or hide the loopholes of) a new capitalist system that generated unmanageable amounts of waste. It is no coincidence that jam exists for that same purpose: turning excess produce (of something rather bitter, in our case) into a more palatable and sustainable consumer good that lasts longer than one season, and in doing so, reduces its waste.

Abdel Nasser and Becoming Samira

A decade later, Widad was married with two boys, pregnant with a girl, and had changed her name to Samira (Susu to her friends). This marked a shift to a softer name that was more en vogue, and it echoed many of her generation's wish to mask their more traditional identities. Her two long braids were replaced with a short curly bob, and her dresses accentuated her silhouette with waist-cinchers and petticoats of puffed nylon. It was the 1950s: The monarchy was dethroned by the 1952 revolution, the last remaining British troops had left Egypt, and Gamal Abdel Nasser's voice was everywhere on the radio. Every Saturday, she would pay a visit to the baqqaal, or grocer, of Manshiyyat al-Bakri, a neighborhood in Heliopolis, Cairo. Then she would pass by a kushk to pick up her weekly copy of *Hawaa'*. *Hawaa'* was the trendy leading women's magazine of the time. It was first published in 1955 by Dar Al Hilal, one of the four main privately owned publishing houses, whose ownership was transferred to the National Union, Nasser's political party, in 1960 as part of a press nationalization movement. **3** The magazine covered topics ranging from beauty and fashion to family and career advice, in addition to home management. Every couple of weeks, a complimentary booklet, titled *Hadaya Hawaa'* (Hawaa' Gifts), was included as a bonus with the magazine. These little booklets of 15 to 20 pages were a window into a world of aspirations. As one of their introductory texts mentioned, they were the "friend" and comrade on which every woman should rely as her guide to modern ways of thinking, behaving, dressing, and most certainly of cooking. Each booklet had its own theme, and every few weeks, a culinary one was published, full of recipes that were written and edited by Bahiya Uthman (another graduate of Berridge House), the co-author of the influential textbook *Usul al-Tahy: al-Nathari w-al-'Amali* (1954), commonly known as Abla Nazira's book.

3 *Hassan, Abdulla. 2016. "Front Row Seat To History: Mohammed Hasanein Heikal." Arab Media Society.*

The magazine was aimed at the housewives of Abdel Nasser's much adored and fast-growing middle class. They lack any mention of cooks, servants, or household help that were a sign of high-income households. The single laundry detergent advertisement on the back cover of some issues is for a local brand, something that would not be targeted at the affluent classes.

Other arts-and-crafts-themed pamphlets featured ideas on sewing and recycling. In some pamphlets, images as well as mentions of household size and number of rooms (two to four bedrooms maximum) are included, showing homes that were typical of middle-class family economic accommodations. In the culinary booklets, a plethora of recipes ask for leftover chicken and breadcrumbs to make salads and meatless stuffings, all of which would be unheard of in aristocratic households. Among the booklets that Widad (now Samira) especially loved is the one titled "Jams":

> "It [jam] plays a central role in the health and the economy, as it's cheap, nutritious, and loved by most people... Its preparation, cooking, and storage is easy. There is an obvious difference between those that are ready-made in stores and the homemade ones."

This is the opening statement of the "Jams" booklet, in which it is hard not to notice the repeated emphasis on its economic aspect, and the attention given to elevating the lifestyle and wellbeing of the middle-class Abdel Nasser adored. The booklet's recipe for the bitter orange jam itself, however, remains the same as the one from Samira's old textbook. The only difference is that, at the time, instead of cooking it over a single wabur, she prepared it using her new four-burner stove that she'd gotten after her marriage, together with a water heater and refrigerator. It's what the novelist Sonallah Ibrahim describes in his novel *Zaat* as the "holy trinity" that Abdel Nasser's programs lured people into acquiring.

As the list of the appliances expanded in Samira's home, so did the size of her family and her financial responsibilities. What helped her make ends meet was the newly launched rations program and the new consumer cooperatives that sprouted up everywhere in the country in the 60s. These ration cards provided her with kitchen staples like flour, oil, and eggs at half the price, and they allowed her to keep some money on the side to purchase the more luxurious ingredients, such as créme Chantilly, vermicelli chocolate, and maraschino cherries. The pamphlets required these ingredients for making European desserts, which typically called for jams as either fillings, toppings, or glazes.

Umm Kulthum's Thursdays

Homemade sugar-dusted petit-fours, dainty sandwiches, and fluffy sponge cakes, all filled with the glistening golden bitter orange jam, were staples at Samira's parties on the first Thursday of each month. These were Umm Kulthum's Thursdays of the 60s. That was when her friends and family would get together in her apartment to watch and listen to Umm Kulthum's live concerts broadcast on their brand-new television. On these Thursdays, she would spend the day in the kitchen, preparing for the arrival of her guests with large rollers in her hair before she coiffed it up into a dramatic bouffant. Every so often, she would send her children with a plate of some of these finger-food desserts to her neighbors. This "floating plate" kept drifting between the neighbors of the building, filled with all sorts of desserts and pastries from one house to another, as every housewife showed off her proud creations—and very rarely gave away her recipes. She believed there was no need to mention that the recipes were from *Hawaa'* when receiving the compliments she typically brushed off with self-deprecating modesty. These compliments, and her reputation for being the

 Continued on page 30

family's and the building's best cook, were the marks of success that paralleled a working woman's promotions. That and being a good mother, of course.

When she was asked, later, if she ever wanted to work and have a job, she answered with a chuckle, "Yes, a singer." And singing was exactly what you would hear her do early in the morning before everyone else woke up:

"يا صباح الخير ياللّي معانا.. ياللّي معانا.. الكروان غنّى و صحّانا.. وصحّانا.."
"Oh good morning to those with us, the nightingale sang and woke us up"

Every day at 6 a.m., she would echo Umm Kulthum's young voice in a song that became a morning hymn to many, as she stood rummaging through her kitchen drawers, or flipping through magazines, looking for new recipes in her little sewing room. The jam would shortly after find its customary place on the table, next to a small bowl of fresh cream, which her children would plow into with toasted bread. A few hours later, the radio would again transmit Umm Kulthum's songs after lunch at five in the evening, and then again later at nine, while the family gathered to have a light dinner. Her songs soon became an escape from an anxious reality. Everywhere, signs that the revolution might have failed were beginning to appear, and soon enough, the love for Abdel Nasser in Samira's heart would quickly wither, after what happened the morning of June 10, 1967.

Early that day, the family woke to the exhilarated voice of the radio host, Ahmed Said, announcing the victory of the Egyptian Army in its war against Israel. This sent Egyptians into a euphoric state, heightened by songs and chants of victory. But when Abdel Nasser's voice broke out on the radio hours later, announcing what was in fact a devastating defeat, everything changed. Samira stood in shock at the sight of her husband screaming out in anger and then breaking down into tears. It was the first and last time anyone saw him cry.

Humiliation and confusion took over all of Egypt, but Samira had a different sort of realization. She became aware of how, in just a second, rigid masculinity could come tumbling down. She noticed how she remained flexible yet rooted throughout this entire ordeal. Things began to change, and people's blindfold of trust in the Nasserist project fell off. Samira's parties soon shrank, becoming smaller in size and lower in budget, as the economy deteriorated with Abdel Nasser's wars and unrealistic dreams. Yet Umm Kulthum's songs still played in the background, albeit with a more nationalist tone to boost morale. And so Samira's bitter orange jam was gradually withdrawn from elaborate desserts in tea-party spreads, to stay within its little reusable glass jars—essential sustenance on the breakfast table.

The Eighties and On

On Samira's first visit to her newlywed daughter's apartment, she presented her with a book and a tin box of sablé biscuits sandwiched with lareng jam. She had carefully wrapped the book in yellow wrapping paper and had kept it safely hidden inside her closet: a copy of Nazira Niqula and Bahiya Uthman's *Usul al-Tahy: al-Nathari w-al-'Amali* for her daughter Salwa (my mother), who would soon move abroad to the newly formed United Arab Emirates with her husband. More than 800 pages of recipes, kitchen tips, and instructions fill its pages. Samira had never taught her daughters cooking the way she was taught. Instead, she would casually let them watch her and help out with getting things out of the fridge, washing dishes, or making salad if they wanted. Their own schools stopped home economics at an early age. Instead, as girls, they were required to do mandatory public service upon finishing their higher education. My aunt was assigned to the nearby family planning center, and my mother to a consumer cooperative. These were the days when the government was trying to contain an explosive population growth rate and to assist families with employment and provisions during an economic depression. Samira hoped this book, taught in schools, discussed in radio shows and even popular plays, would be her daughter's guide to figuring out the kitchen while far away from her.

Every following summer, her daughter would return to Egypt loaded with brown jars of Carnation Coffee-Mate for Samira, which Egypt lacked because of strict import control policies. In exchange, she would go back to the United Arab Emirates with six jars of jam, the fruit of which she could not find in the markets of the Arabian desert. With the jam, Samira would give Salwa some of her newly discovered "international" recipes, which she wrote down after watching cooking shows on television. Salwa kept her mother's recipe notes, usually written on the backs of tearaway calendar pages, in between the pages of Abla Nazira and Bahiya Uthman's book. For years, the book stayed in a small black cupboard that moved with the different homes her daughter had, but it always remained in close proximity to the kitchen, at hand whenever needed. With time, it lost its cover, and some of its pages fell apart.

After her husband's death, Samira stayed behind in her apartment in Alexandria, where her family gathered on Fridays, for Eid, and for birthdays. Her fridge started to welcome ready-made strawberry and raspberry jams, and her kitchen counter featured a constant stream of boxes of petits fours from the nearby bakery. Yet she aggressively resisted store-bought cakes and preferred to make her own Greek pastafrolla pie every weekend, until shortly before her own passing. And when she made the pie during the months that followed winter, she typically took out that one jar at the back of the fridge to spread on the pie's top a good layer of the chunky, tangy citrus preserve, which was always part of her kitchen.

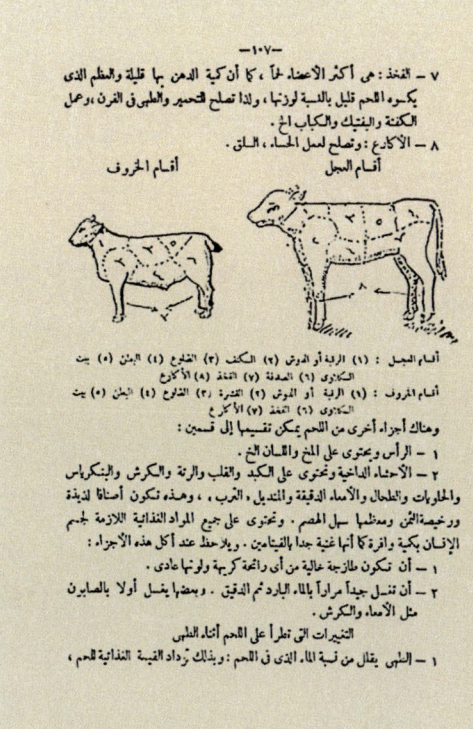

From Uusl al-Tahy, by Abla Nazira

My Fifteen Jars

Staring at the 15 jars in my fridge, I wonder what it would be like if they were sold in some rustic organic farmer's market and labelled "Granny's Bitter Orange Jam" in English. It would probably sell like hotcakes, attracting more people than my best friends and husband, who were clearly lacking in taste. I take out the open jar and scoop a couple of spoonfuls into a saucer. I turn up the fire on the stove and toast my baladi bread quickly on both sides, so that it is slightly charred by the flame. The smokey toasted bits of bread are the best accompaniment to fresh, cold cream. I pour my tea, Syrian Zhourat, and put everything on a small tray, then head to the balcony.

As I sit in a shady corner, dipping into the jam while my Cocker Spaniel eyes every bite, I recall how impatient I was when peeling all the oranges one by one, inconvenienced by how I couldn't touch my phone with sticky fingers to check my notifications. "Shred the peel very thinly so it is almost transparent," the recipe says. And shred and peel the oranges I did, as well as the tip of my finger. I then had to soak the peels for 12 hours, twice, and google words and measurements from the recipe that are no longer in use. Have you ever heard of Alexandrian *magour* (الماجور الاسكندراني) and *agana*? Me neither, nor had my mother or aunts, but thanks to a friend, I learned they were both types of large, deep earthenware pots used for cooking and storing food. This sent me deep down into a rabbit hole on the use of pottery and its different types in old Egyptian cooking. While I do not have a magour or agana, I own a large beautiful earthenware biram with a lid in which I usually store clarified butter, and which I put to work for this 24-hour soak. And so, after soaking, resoaking, straining, simmering, skimming and sterilizing jars, this jam-making process made me approach teita's memory in a slightly different light.

Almost all my memories of her are while she was cooking in the kitchen, making beautiful creations that catered to every family member's cravings and desires. Naturally, I grew up assuming that her relationship with the kitchen was nothing but a passionate hobby and that the immeasurable sum of hours she spent making food for her family was all out of selflessness. But reading through the cookbooks she left behind has given me a broader context to her life, which situates her culinary experience in the heart of gender, political, social, and economic struggles. It is easy to over-romanticize our grandmothers and their food, as we see everywhere nowadays with commercializing and marketing the teita/grandma/nonna figure. Yet their ties to food are often over-simplified in the name of "generosity," "selflessness," and "unconditional love." Their experience is glossed over with a certain naivety and nostalgia that is divorced from the realities of their time, as if one can take any woman from any time and her relationship to food and the kitchen would be the same universally.

What I found between the lines of her cookbooks, on the back of her newspaper recipe clippings, and in her collection of women's magazines, are stories of the heavy expectations placed on women, modernist aspirations, and financial hardships. My image of her became much more complicated, nuanced by her own struggle with making a family, maintaining a "happy" home, and cutting corners to better save. But more than anything, it made me think of the person beyond her domestic duties, obligations, and expectations—even if they were self-imposed. It made me think of her as a little girl receiving lessons in how to make steamed ginger puddings like countless other girls in the first half of the 20th century, in schools operating under a colonial British ideology of "elevating" women. I pictured her flipping through the cookbooks, selecting which hors d'oeuvres might impress her neighboring working wives, as a way of proving that she, too, could be successful staying at home. It made me think of how she sat budgeting every month's

۳۳

groceries as the country's economy went spiraling downhill, as it funded wars and unrealistic nation-building projects. And in an unforeseen way, this jam brought me closer to an understanding of Egypt's story. A bittersweet one that I have returned to, to live and continue, after my mother left 30 years ago. A story of a country and its people that is layered with nuances as rich and complex as the flavors and textures that meet in lareng.

Today, as I sit savoring the citrusy preserve, I acknowledge the privilege I have: the ability to make choices, as a woman. I have no doubt that she truly loved cooking—it would have been impossible to garner such a legacy in the kitchen if she did not truly have a passion for it. Still, I believe she might have been someone else entirely if it wasn't for external and social factors. One thing remains true, though: what she left behind of her life, including her recipes and her cookbooks, amount to so much more than a reduced image of the grandmother. The greater part of her life was heavily influenced by factors she did not choose. And it is in this quiet acceptance of the mundane, the ordinary, and the dull—over what she could have been, if things had been different—that real strength lies. The tiresome task of thinly and meticulously peeling the bitter orange, soaking its peel repeatedly for 24 hours, then cutting, juicing, straining, and sweetening something that is otherwise too sour and bitter to the taste, over and over and over again. It is an act of persevering, of sustaining herself and her loved ones through hardship, and of finding some sweetness within her life—when perhaps all she wanted was to heal Egypt's shattered hopes after Abdel Nasser, and to sing on the radio with Umm Kulthum.

۳۵

Poetry

My Mother's Kitchen

By Rym Jalil

Translated by Mariam Boctor

Every day I lie and say
I know this place.
My mother's kitchen
brims with afflictions
I must pretend to befriend it
we all know it can have only one master
from its beginning to its end

A holy place that's hard to visit
every single confrontation within its walls.
A few hours of truthful conversation
but mostly, a landscape of fights

Why isn't it a duty to narrate the past
as part of a thousand present realities?
Why isn't it my right to share my story
(as a cornerstone of stories)?

The arrangement of her spices
shows she will not budge.
Would it hurt if there were space
for two?
It's less an issue of space
than of spanning differences—
even if you could yield
your ego would resist.
It would be too much to be expelled
from your kingdom.

Every day
I lie and say I know this place.
My mother's kitchen
brims with afflictions
the map is complicated, annotated:
there's a border guard
if you submit and acquiesce,
your stay may be extended

كل يوم أضحك على نفسي
وأقول عارفاه
مطبخ أمي المليان مشي سيعاه
لازم بناء علاقة سطحة مع واحد
اكيدنه ليه سيد واحد
من بداية الأمر لنهايته

مكان مقدس صعب زيارته
حيث كل المواجهات
ساعات حوادث حقيقية
والعادي ساحة خلافات

ليه مش واجب سرد الماضي
كجزء من واقع الزقات
ليه مش من حقك تشارك
(كحجر أساسي في الحكايات)

فهمت من رصة بهاراتها
إنها محكماها حتتين
كان هيجرى ايه لو فيه مكان
لاثنين
الأزمة مش في المساحات
لكن في احتواء الاختلافات
إن كنت ناوي ع القبول
ضميرك هتحاسبك
أصل مش من الاصول
تطرد من مملكتك

كل يوم أضحك على نفسي
وأقول عارفاه
مطبخ أمي المليان مشي سيعاه
خريطته معقدة ومفرككة
وعليه ضابط مرور
لو انسيت قصاده
ممكن تاخد تأشيرة عبور

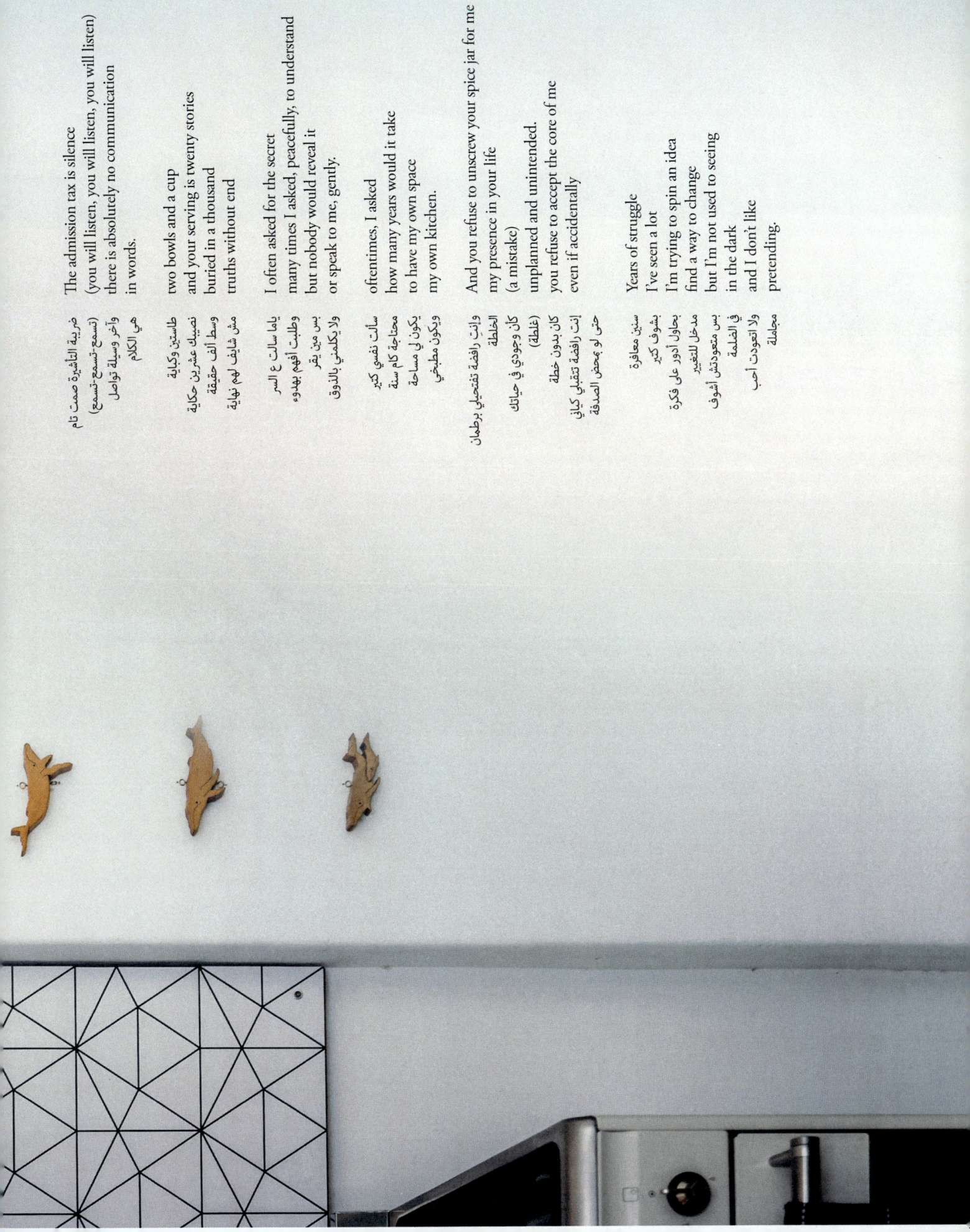

The admission tax is silence
(you will listen, you will listen, you will listen)
there is absolutely no communication
in words.

two bowls and a cup
and your serving is twenty stories
buried in a thousand
truths without end

I often asked for the secret
many times I asked, peacefully, to understand
but nobody would reveal it
or speak to me, gently.

oftentimes, I asked
how many years would it take
to have my own space
my own kitchen.

And you refuse to unscrew your spice jar for me
my presence in your life
(a mistake)
unplanned and unintended.
you refuse to accept the core of me
even if accidentally

Years of struggle
I've seen a lot
I'm trying to spin an idea
find a way to change
but I'm not used to seeing
in the dark
and I don't like
pretending.

غريبة الثانية صمت تام
(تسمع-تسمع-تسمع)
وآخر وسيلة تواصل
هي الكلام

طاستين وكباية
نصيبك عشرين حكاية
وسط ألف حقيقة
مش شايف لهم نهاية

يما سألت ع السر
وطلبت أفهم بهدوء
بس مين ٭ ٭ ٭
ولا يكلمني بالذوق

سألت نفسي كتير
محتاجة كام سنة
يكون لي مساحة
ويكون مطبخي

وإنت رافضة تفتحيلي برطمان
الخلطة
(غلطة)
كان وجودي في حياتك
كان بدون خطة
إنت رافضة تتقبلي كياني
حتى لو بعض الصدفة

سنين معافرة
بشوف كتير
بحاول أدور على فكرة
مدخل للتغيير
بس متعودتش أشوف
في الضلمة
ولا اتعودت أحب
مجاملة

Poetry

A Kitchen of My Own

By **Rym Jalil**

Translated by Mariam Boctor

I've memorized my new kitchen
every single corner of it's loved:
walls embrace
and plates hold.
It takes me as I am
and my meals are enough

In my own kitchen there are no restrictions
on screwing up
on daydreaming
or on my own time inventing recipes
to relish.

I dance freely with the salt
I chance upon truths that ease my heart
my coffee at dawn
tickles my brain
with just the right roast

I'm no longer afraid of the chili pepper
and eat it on my own terms.
I welcome it
even in moments of trouble
I take a breath
(deeply)
and my tongue tastes the lesson.

The day I slightly burned the oil
I treated myself
to stuffed kunafa.
Punishments now are my own to decide.
I plump my soul,
give her gifts galore.

مطبخي الجديد أنا حافظة
عارفة كل ركن فيه وحبه
حيطانه بتحضن
أطباقه بتحتوي
واخدني زي ما أنا
ووجباتي مكتفية

في مطبخي الجديد مفيش موانع
إني أغلط
إني أسرح
وعلى وقتي الخاص اخترع
وصفات تفرح

رقصت مع الملح بحرية
اكتشفت حقائق تثلج ضميري
قهوتي في ساعة صبحية
تروق على دماغي
بالتحميصة اللي هي

معودتش أخاف من الشطة
بقيت أكلها وراحتي
بل وبرحب بيها كتكرة
حتى في لحظات الضيق
باخد نفس
(عميق)
ولساني بدوق العبرة

يوم ما حرقت الزيت شوية
كافئت نفسي بكنافة محشية
أصل عقابي دلوقتي قراري
وأحببني هدية

٤٠/40

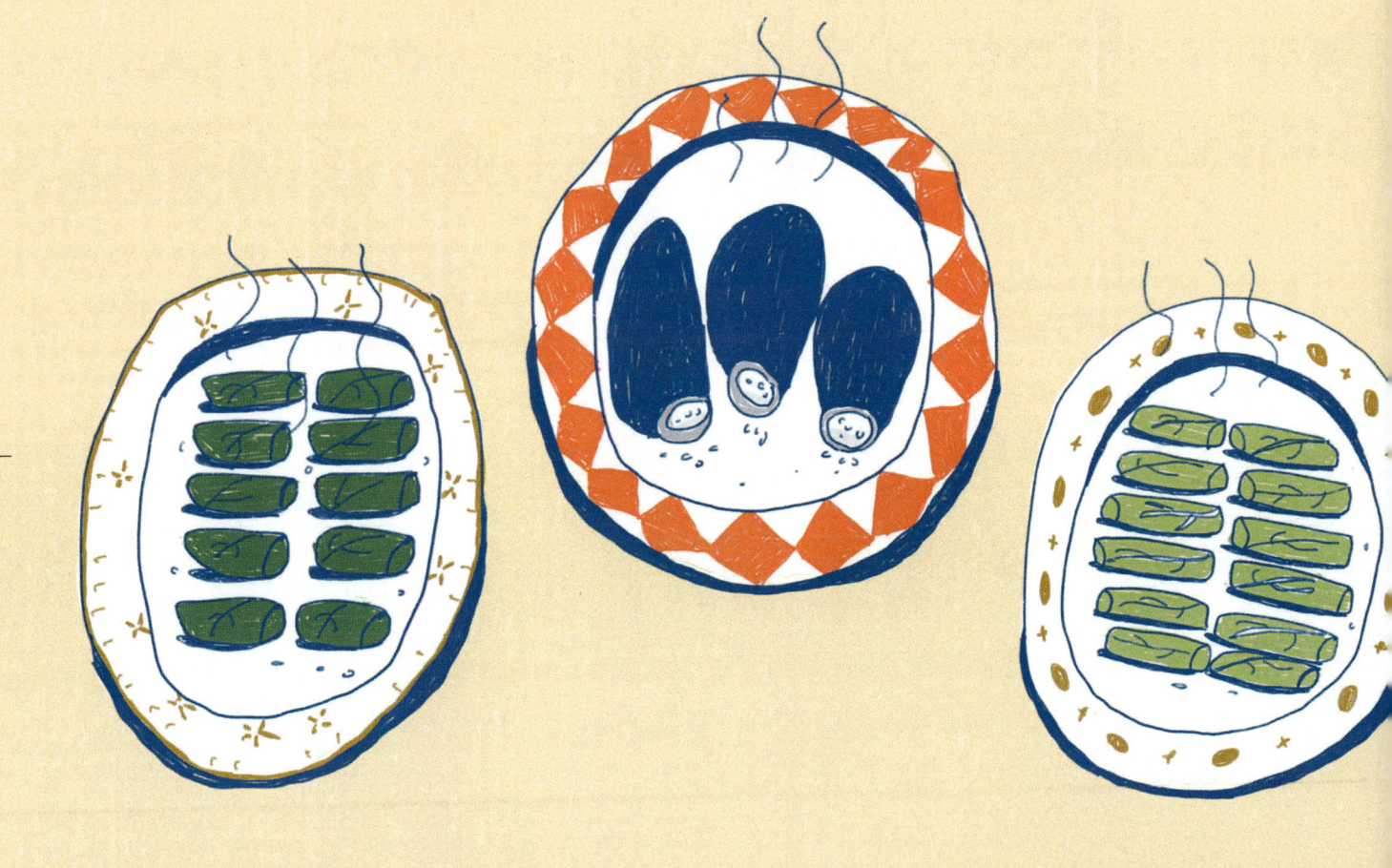

Graphic Novel

المحشي

Making Mahshi

By **Sohila Khaled**

In the following series of illustrations, Sohila Khaled playfully depicts her steps for preparing one of her favorite meals, a staple of traditional Egyptian food: *Mahshi!*

The ingredients to be stuffed are: 1) Grape leaves, 2) Eggplant, cored, 3) Zucchini, cored, 4) Cabbage, boiled with cumin and salt, cut into rectangles, 5) Tomato, cored, 6) Bell pepper, cored.

التسبيكة

The sauce and flavoring for the rice (*tasbeekah*) requires:
1) Tomato juice, boiled down to a thick paste, as well as 2) Chopped onions,
3) Ghee, 4) Oil, 5) Cumin,
6) Coriander, 7) Salt,
8) Pepper.

The rice must be washed, drained, and added to your sauce on low heat, and the greens—fresh parsley, fresh cilantro, and fresh dill—should be added to the rice and sauce. The resulting stuffing mixture should be stuffed into all ingredients except for the grape leaves and cabbage, which need to be hand-rolled.

الأرزّ

الخُضْرَة

شِبِت   كُسْبِرَة   بَقْدونِس

الخُضْرَة
+
أُرز والسَّمَكة

الحشو

٤٦/46

ولف المحشي

لمدة ساعة
على نار هادئة

"مرقة"

As for the cooking: Line and pack your rolled mahshi tightly together in a pot, place your stuffed mahshi on top or in the middle facing up, add stock or broth, and cook on a low heat for an hour or until rice is cooked through. Enjoy!

محشي الباذنجان محشي الكرنب

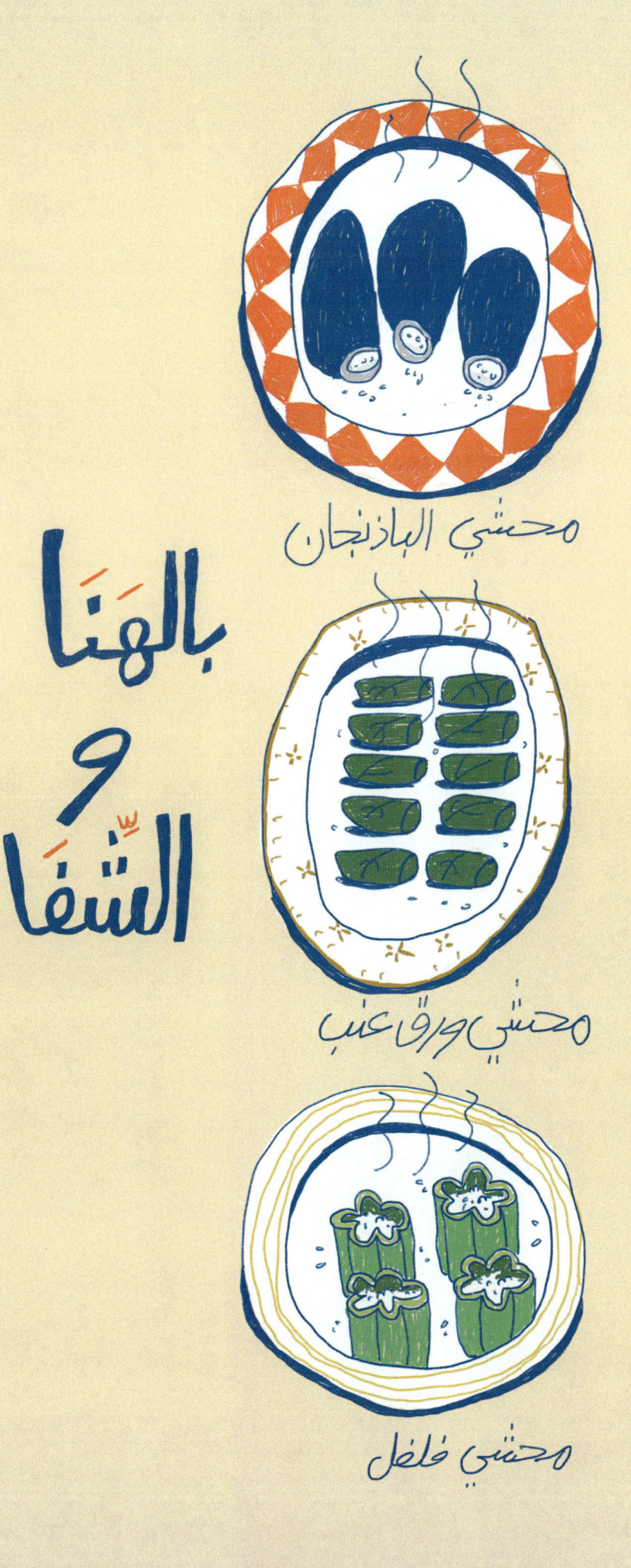

بالهَنَا
و
الشِّفَا

محشي ورق عنب محشي الكوسة

محشي فلفل محشي طماطم

SYRIAN WOMEN   3980-14

Essay

'It Was to Her a Ritual'

Domesticity and the Making of Syrian American Culture

By **Zaina Ujayli**

"The glowing coals in the grate made the kitchen pleasantly warm.
On top of the stove, the coffee bubbled tempestuously in the percolator. To one side was a frying-pan in which eggs were sizzling in olive oil.
On the table was a dish of fat, juicy olives which had ripened in some Syrian grove; a dish of laban, and one of dates stewed in sugar. There were small, flat disks of Syrian bread, baked especially for Khalil.
Mariam did not like to see him making cartwheel slices of American bread, which he did by removing the inner part and eating the crust ."

Edna K. Saloomey, "A Party for Aneesa", *The Syrian World*

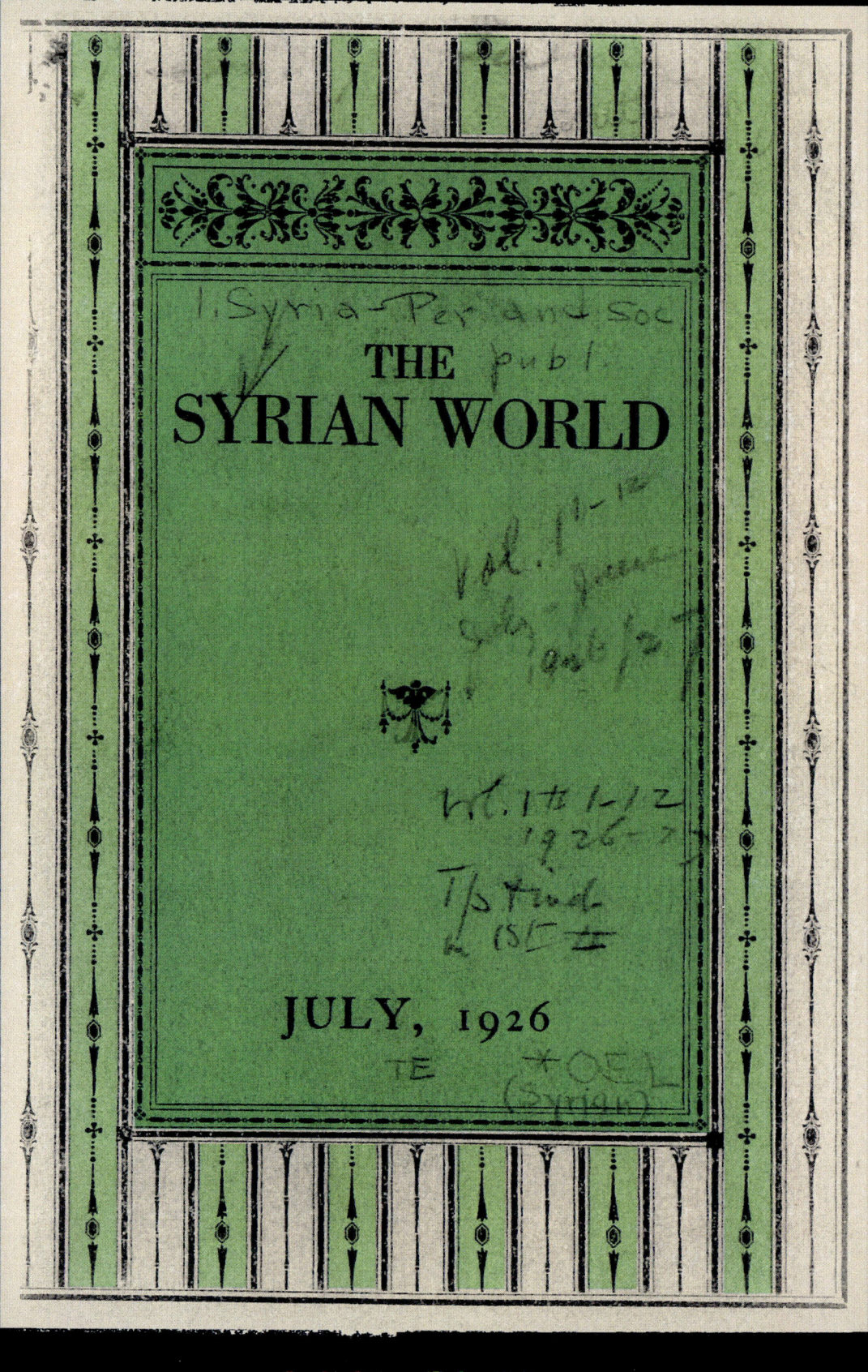

THE SYRIAN WORLD

JULY, 1926

One of the first issues of The Syrian World

You wouldn't call the description of the Arab-American kitchen in the passage above remarkable. The images the author renders are familiar, maybe not only on the page, but in your own kitchen. As you were reading, you might have given the olives the color of the olives you keep in your pantry. You could have imagined the laban in your fridge, the brand that, though you can now find it at your regional grocery chain, you still buy cheaper at your go-to Syrian or Palestinian or Iraqi store.

But here's the thing—I want you to read the description of this Arab American kitchen as remarkable, radical even, because it captures the domestic, the familiar, and precisely because it makes you think of the olives in your pantry.

The description comes from Saloomey's short story "A Party for Aneesa," printed in 1931 in the English-language magazine *The Syrian World*. The magazine's editor introduces Saloomey as "an American-born Syrian girl in whom the call of our blood is manifested in such tender ways for the country of our parents." In addition to publishing short stories and poetry in *The Syrian World*, Saloomey would become the editor of the magazine's column "Our Younger Generation" the same year she wrote "A Party for Aneesa." In one of her first columns, she addressed the dilemma of the earliest generations of Arab Americans:

Salloum Mokarzel, editor of The Syrian World. National Museum of American History

"We are wedged tightly between tradition and experiment. Always there has been a struggle between these two to conquer, but for us, who have been transplanted into surroundings entirely new, the battle has been keener than any before. We are at a loss whether to succumb to tradition, or die for experiment. There are some of us to whom the experience has been so overwhelming as to cause their reason to be dazed; and they wander about with an expression like that of Elihu Vedder's painting, 'The Sorrowing Soul Between Doubt and Faith.' In our case, we have been wandering in a desert partly of our own creation and partly a creation of circumstance."

To be wandering in a desert of both circumstance and one's own creation was a fitting metaphor for being Arab in America in the early twentieth century. The waves of immigration at the end of the nineteenth and in the early twentieth centuries created not only burgeoning Arab immigrant communities from Louisiana to Chicago, among whom writers like Afifa Karam and Gibran Khalil Gibran flourished, but a new generation of American-born Arabs to live in what we might call the crossroads of those immigrant communities.

The Sorrowing Soul Between Doubt and Faith

Despite their legally "white" categorization and the community's overall effort to assimilate, Arabs, most arriving from then-Ottoman Syria, were often still viewed as "exotic." Consequently, in an effort to lose their "foreign" quality, young Arabs distanced themselves from their parents and the "old world," resisting learning

LITTLE SYRIA, NY

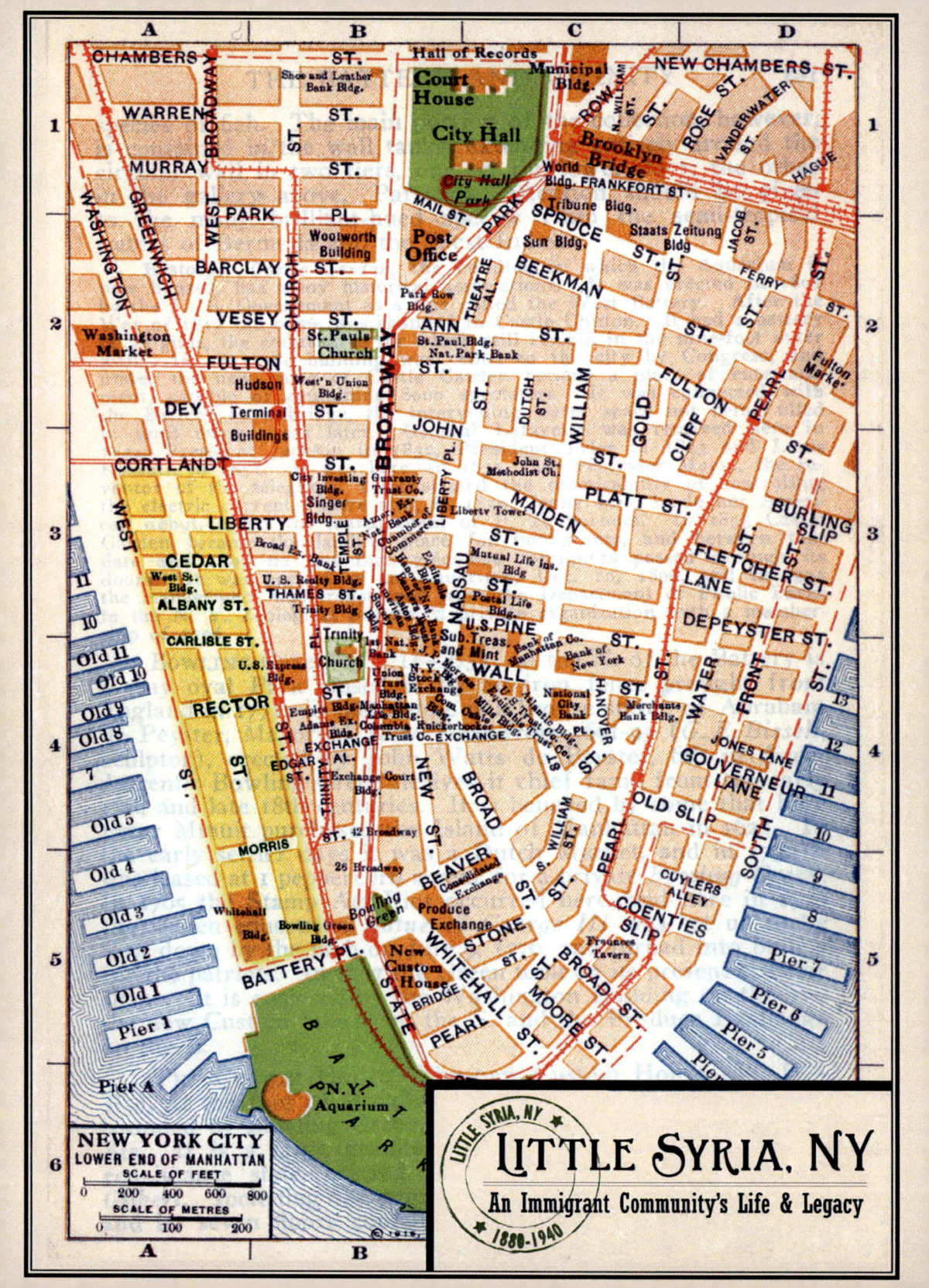

An Immigrant Community's Life & Legacy

Little Syria, NY · 1880–1940

NEW YORK CITY — LOWER END OF MANHATTAN

Arabic, refusing to cook traditional food, and abandoning cultural practices. Writer Evelyn Shakir argued that it was because American-born children "costumed themselves as 'regular Americans' and hoped to pass" that we have so little early Arab American literature. As a result, young Arab Americans became not only isolated, both by choice and circumstance, from the immigrant communities in which they lived, but also silenced.

It is this isolated, silent figure Saloomey identifies with in Elihu Vedder's "The Sorrowing Soul Between Doubt and Faith." That Saloomey chooses Vedder is itself a statement. The New York-born painter became famous for his illustrations for Edward Fitzgerald's 1884 edition of Omar Khayyam's *Rubaiyat*. Like the American edition of Khayyam's poems, collected, painted, translated, and published in America, but indebted to the Persian original, the woman at the forefront of "The Sorrowing Soul Between Doubt and Faith" is caught between the gaze of two worlds. At her back, two people watch her, but she does not look back at them. She looks ahead with what Saloomey identifies as a "dazed" expression, and stands alone, shadowed despite her frontal position. For Saloomey, this is the woman who represented the stance of the first American-born Arabs—a lonely figure standing lost and alone between the watchful, expectant eyes of both her inherited Arab culture and American birthright.

Published between 1926–1932, *The Syrian World* was an American periodical uniquely conceived to address the very issue of Arab American youths' identity struggles. Its chief editor, Salloum Mokarzel, writes in the forward to the periodical's first volume: "The somewhat anomalous position of the young Syrian in America constitutes a genuine social problem pressing for a solution, and it is both to his own interest and to that of the country under whose flag he was born that the correction of this condition should not be further delayed." His "correction" was *The Syrian World*: a periodical that functioned like a hand-picked manual of everything an American child needed to know about the Arab world. From Arabic aphorisms to photographs of sites across Syria and the Middle East, *The Syrian World* provided American-born children an extensive education on the history, literature, and politics of Syria and the Arab world. The purpose behind this education was to convince Arab American children to embrace both their Arab heritage and American birthright, and, in so doing, address the crisis of their identity.

However, *The Syrian World* published remarkably few stories about Arab Americans in their day-to-day lives. The periodical paired original poems and content with translations of classical Arabic poems and folktales, mostly focused on the Middle East. Even as editors advocated for Arab Americans to embrace life as both Arab and American and reconcile themselves to their "anomalous position," they did not narrate in their fictions how that life might look. Instead, male writers contributed adventurous stories which often took place overseas, from murder tales to palace dramas. Chances are you might recognize a few of *The Syrian World*'s male contributors, whose names include the Mokarzel brothers, Ameen Rihani, and Khalil Gibran, who have all been memorialized in discussions of *The Syrian World*. The female writers who published alongside them, however, have been left behind in the archive.

THE SYRIAN-AMERICAN PRESS
104 GREENWICH ST.,
NEW YORK

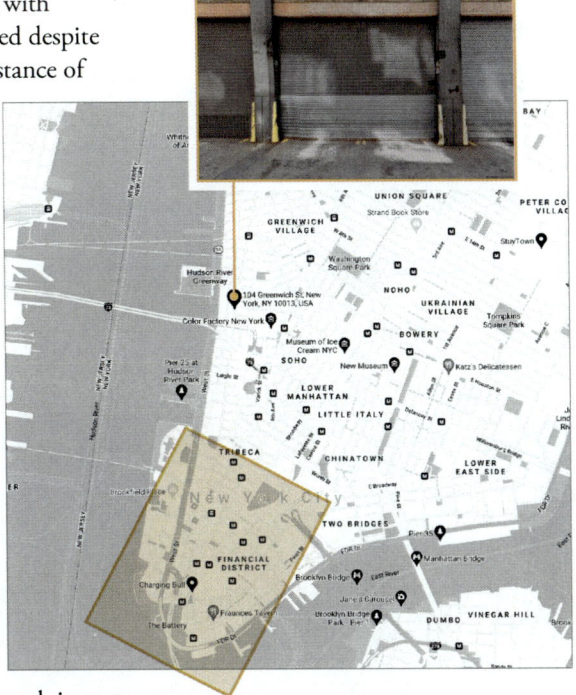

The location where The Syrian World was printed. Framed: Little Syria

Syrian pastry cook,
Lower Image: Syrian peddlers in Lower Manhattan
© Library of Congress

And yet it was female writers who composed the most identifiably Arab American literature within the pages of *The Syrian World*. While men rarely wrote about Arab Americans, and even more rarely still set their stories in America, young American-born Arab women, like Labeebee A.J. Hanna and Saloomey, published short stories that took place in Arab American kitchens and living rooms.

Consider this: like the stories published by her male peers, Hanna's short story "Isaf" (published in *The Syrian World* in 1929) tells an Arab legend about a Bedouin man who realizes his wife has cheated on him, and, after killing a wolf for his in-laws, learns that they killed her. While the story is a darkly misogynist tale of honor killing, unlike other legends published in *The Syrian World*, it is comically embedded within Arab American life. Hanna assumes the point of view of two young Arab American girls hearing the tale from their father and uncle in a kitchen. Because the girls do not fully understand Arabic, the telling of the dark tale is rife with children's questions and misinterpretations, and ends with the girls asking to have Arabic expressions explained to them. Consequently, while "Isaf" tells the story of an Arab legend and includes Arabic songs, the emphasis is instead on how the girls are inheriting it in their American kitchen.

Writers like Saloomey and Hanna often lingered on these everyday particularities of constructing the crossroads of immigrant life, of homes constructed between America and the Arab diaspora, and the people traversing both. Whether that meant joining Arab American girls listening to an Arab legend in their kitchen, or describing Arab American children singing Arabic songs in the car, or watching a young couple exchanging a translated copy of the *Rubaiyat*—Saloomey and Hanna's stories highlighted how and where Arab cultural practices were maintained in America. Even as Saloomey wrote about the crisis of identity faced by her generation, she and young Arab American writers like Hanna set out to prove in their fiction that life at the crossroads of embattled nationalisms was possible, and that this war was often fought in the kitchen.

In Saloomey's story, "A Party for Aneesa," the protagonist Mariam is described as a "delectable housewife" who takes great care to appear "ultra modern" for her professional husband, and is proud that she knows enough English to read the newspapers. Her desire to learn English and claim American modernity might make her seem like a character obsessed with assimilation—but she is far from it. Instead, from Mariam's bustling in the kitchen, Saloomey renders the portrait of an Arab woman carefully constructing her American domestic space. Mariam keeps olives from Syria, but practices reading English newspapers. She styles herself in a modern way, but bakes Syrian bread by hand for her family.

Professor Susan Fraiman tells us to imagine the domestic space as both constructed and affected. What that means is that the things we take for granted, that we see as normal and everyday have agency and intention behind them. This is especially true of immigrant households. Fraiman writes: "in first-generation households, the preservation of old-country identity results not from a passive traditionalism or refusal to assimilate but instead from the active, daily regeneration of this identity, usually by women, through physically demanding and affectively charged rituals of cooking, dress, and housekeeping." In other words, immigrant women often stand at the center of cultural assimilation and cultural preservation.

*The Lebanon Restaurant,
88 Washington Street, 1936,
New York Public Library*

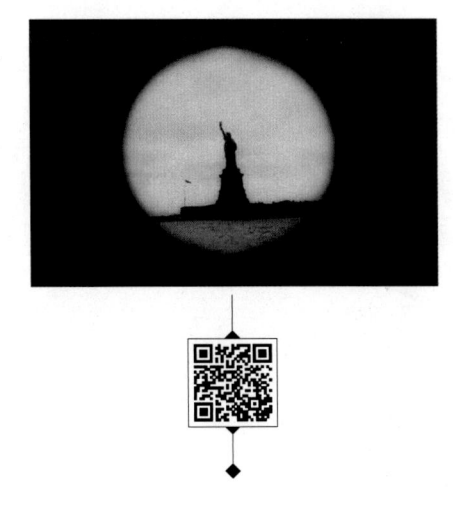

*From "Najib Diab Arrives In New York
-1893"*

Woman modeling shirtwaists for Assi Sheheen's factory, 1919.
The Syrian American Commercial Magazine

شهر كانون الاول سنة ١٩١٨ الصفحة السابعة والاربعون

محل عاصي شاهين واولاده

١٩١٣ وست اخر موضة جورجات مكسرة ومخرجة بازرار جميلة. سعر ٣،٧٥

١٩٠٩ اجمل موضة واثقل جورجات مطرزة بحرير وخرز قبة ملورة ورائجة كثيرا. سعر ٥،٧٥

Syrian children playing in the street in New York City.
Library of Congress

For this reason, writers like Saloomey and Hanna frequently placed Arab American women at the forefront of their narratives. In "A Party for Aneesa," the emphasis on the kitchen and the home highlights the role women play in preserving Arab cultural practices for their families. The "party" Mariam wants to put on is for her daughter Aneesa to encourage her to meet and marry a Syrian boy and, as a result, remain connected to a community that visits their home and gives toasts in Arabic. Saloomey's narrative is, rather than a story in which Mariam works to assimilate or even completely preserve her Arab heritage, a story in which Mariam strives to construct a dynamic, modern interpretation of a hybrid Arab American home for her family. Saloomey painstakingly describes the ritual of a mother and housewife maintaining her family's heritage, and thus speaks to the practice of cultural maintenance that is echoed in every diaspora kitchen.

But let's return to Fraiman's word "ritual," which Saloomey also uses in "A Party for Aneesa." When Saloomey describes Mariam cooking for her family, Saloomey writes that the "task was done not from a sense of duty; it was to her a ritual." Rituals evoke tradition and familiarity, but also something sacred. Maybe that is why in his 1925 column describing the Arab enclave in New York City, journalist Jean Piper writes for the *Brooklyn Daily Eagle* that "Syrian Bread is Sacred." He describes the bakeries on Washington Street and the bakery boys dropping off circles of bread on every doorstep. "The Syrian housewife has a standing order with her baker, the same as an American woman with her dairyman," Piper writes. "To the Syrian, bread is a sacred food. Children are taught not to throw it on the ground and to kiss it if it falls from their hands." Baking bread, making Syrian food, maintaining cultural cuisines, is one of the easiest ways to maintain and evolve cultural practices in America. The kitchen is the nexus of that space, a place to share stories, to share food; that it has been historically coded as a feminine space speaks to women's agency at the vanguard of preserving one way of life while surrounded by and adapting to another. In the daily construction and transference of culture in diaspora, bread from back home is more than bread. It is a living example of cultural diaspora in the making.

While the construction of an Arab American domesticity might be deemed unremarkable, in the context in which Hanna and Saloomey were writing, it was radical, an important cultural and historical marker. At a time in which Arab Americans were struggling to define what it looked like to live as an Arab American, Hanna and Saloomey supplied examples. In the writing they left behind, they narrated some of the earliest experiences of being Syrian women in America. "We have been wandering in a desert partly of our own creation," Saloomey wrote of her generation, "and partly a creation of circumstance." And yet, in spite of their struggle to define themselves, they planted in that desert the first seeds of Arab American literature.

Saloomey's and Hanna's kitchen spaces are remarkable because, at first, you likely wouldn't read them as remarkable. However, it was the agency and intention behind the formation of Arab American kitchens in the 1930s that normalized and provided a blueprint for the ever-evolving picture of seemingly unremarkable Arab American kitchens today. The choices we make every day, even choices as routine as buying olives, baking bread, and spreading laban in a small dish, have the power in diaspora to maintain culture, introduce traditions, and destigmatize the various ways life can be lived in the midst of multiple cultures.

The Brooklyn Daily Eagle, Sunday, Jan 18, 1925, page 60

Excerpt

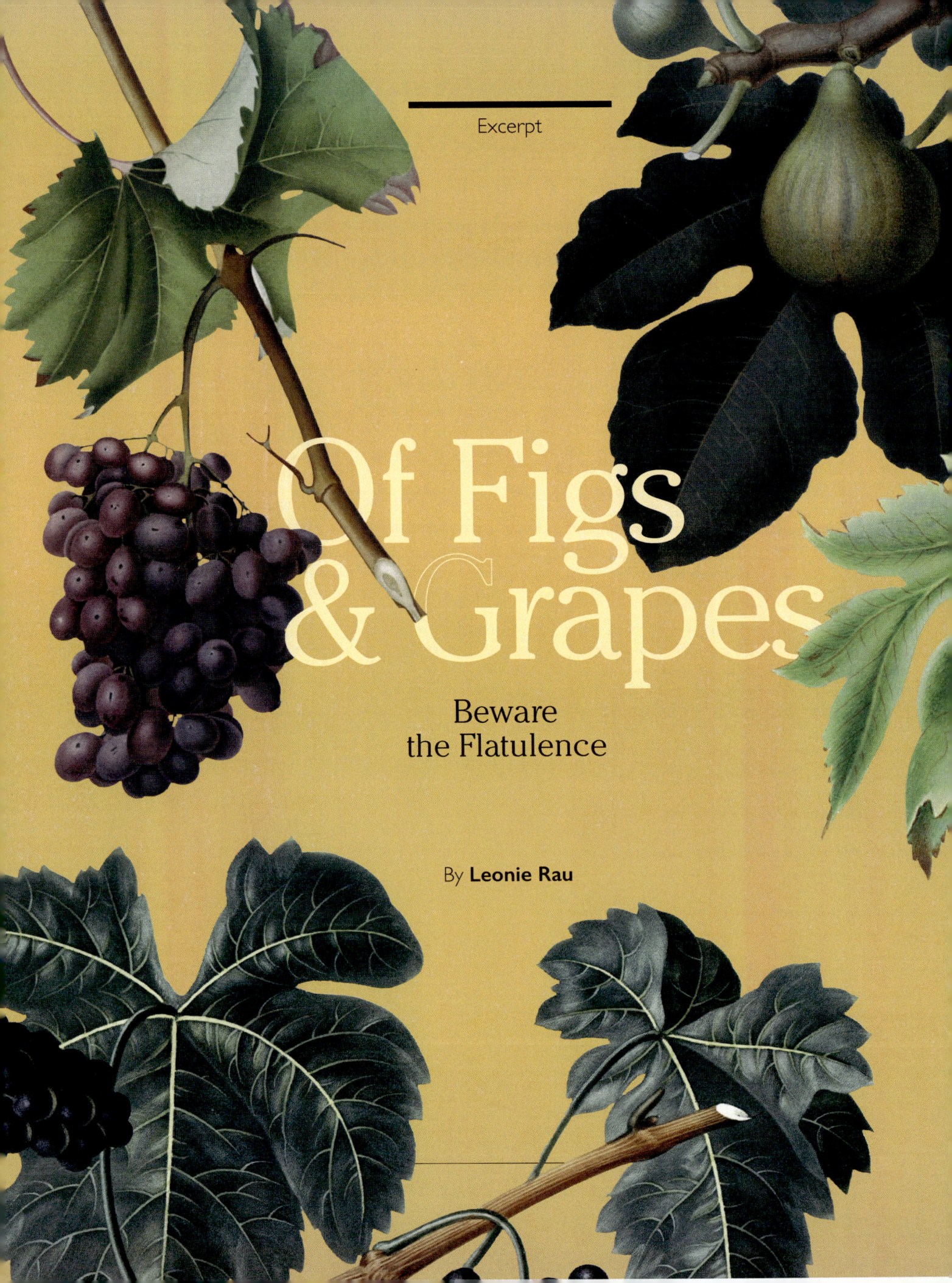

Of Figs & Grapes

Beware the Flatulence

By **Leonie Rau**

بسم الله الرّحمن الرّحيم

جالينوس يقول في التين والعنب إنهما سيدا الفواكه [1]

"Galen says, of figs and grapes, that they are the lords of the fruits."

Thus begins the chapter on fruit in Andalusi physician Abu Marwan 'Abd al-Malik Ibn Zuhr's (d. 1162 CE) *Kitab al-Aghdhiya* (Book of Foodstuffs), which belongs to a rich and well-documented body of dietetic works composed in Arabic between the ninth and 16th centuries.

Most medieval Arabic medical texts, including this one, are predicated upon a theory of humors, a concept widely used in many parts of the world, from Antiquity to the 19th century. Its most well-known model, described by Hippocrates and systematized by Galen, is that of the four humors or juices, and their respective qualities, which need to be balanced in order to achieve an even temperament and a healthy body. Those humors are blood, yellow bile, black bile, and phlegm. Each corresponds to two of the four qualities: heat, cold, humidity, and dryness. Foods were thought to skew toward one of these qualities, thus influencing the equilibrium of bodily humors. They could also be used to counterbalance excesses or deficiencies of the humors.

In his *Kitab al-Aghdhiya*, Ibn Zuhr lists various foodstuffs organized by category and describes the food's humoral properties, its medical uses and benefits, as well as its potential harmful effects. One is a mouthwateringly long list of fruits that includes apples, pears, pomegranates, quinces, peaches, various citrus fruits, and berries, as well as the abovementioned highly praised figs and grapes.

[1] Abu Marwan 'Abd al-Malik Ibn Zuhr, Kitab al-Agdiya (Tratado de los Alimentos), tr. Expiración Garciá Sánchez (Madrid: Consejo Superior de Investigaciones Científicas, 1992), p. 43.

He writes on figs:

Figs are hot and humid; they upset the stomach and soften the belly. They possess useful benefits due to their sweetness and milkiness. The best of them are the ones that have ripened entirely; the worst are the unripe.

The dried ones are less humid and much hotter than the fresh ones, and they are either balanced between dryness and humidity—while leaning slightly towards dryness—or else are dry, yet not excessively so.

They upset the stomach less and also soften the belly less, and cause far less flatulence than the fresh ones, although they are not entirely flatulence-free during their digestion; it's only that they are also produced in the belly and in what else there is.

They provide healthy nourishment that fattens if it is eaten regularly and calms the irascible faculty that is in the heart and diminishes it in particular. From it—after its digestion—there remains residue in the organs from which develop head lice by the power of God the Exalted.

Unfortunately, Ibn Zuhr is silent on how exactly the eating of figs may lead to lice, but, as most contemporary science confirms, he was right about the flatulence.

Figs are thought to have been cultivated in West Asia, specifically the Jordan Valley, for more than 11,000 years, and have had an outsized significance. In the first book of the Hebrew Bible, Adam and Eve cover themselves with fig leaves after becoming aware of their nakedness once they eat from the tree of knowledge (Gen. 1:3). The ninety-fifth sura of the Qur'an, *Surat al-Teen*, begins with the words "by the fig and the olive!" Here, the fig can stand either for Damascus and the ancient region of Greater Syria, or for Mount Judi, the alleged resting place of Noah's Ark on today's border between Turkey and Syria, according to the exegetes cited by Ibn Kathir. [2]

Despite this great cultural import, the fig is conspicuously absent from extant medieval Arabic cookery books: Ibn Sayyar al-Warraq's tenth-century cookbook from Baghdad mentions (dried) figs mainly as a garnish and for their laxative properties if consumed before meals, while an anonymous 13th-century Andalusi manuscript describes a recipe for fig syrup.

However, much as Adam and Eve sought to preserve their dignity by covering up with fig leaves, they are most often called for to wrap and preserve fruits such as quinces, apples, and grapes. Commenting on recipes contained in the thirteenth-century cookbooks *Wusla ila l-habib fi wasf al-tayyibat wa-al-tibb* and the *Kitab al-Tabikh*, Maxime Rodinson argues that ingredients such as figs were perhaps "thought too commonplace" to merit mention. [3] Perhaps they were also mostly consumed separately, rather than being used in dishes and beverages.

In comparison, the second "lord" of the fruits, the grape, is far more present in a wide variety of recipes. Ibn Zuhr writes:

Fig Tree
Walters Art Museum, Baltimore
W.659 folio: 207v
Turkey unspec., c. 1717
(al-Qazwini, Zakariya; 'Aja'ib al-makhluqat)

[2] *Ibn Kathir, Tafsir al-Qur'an al-'azim (Beirut: Dar al-Fikr, 1981). Vol. 4, p. 526.*

[3] *Maxime Rodinson, „Studies in Arabic Manuscripts Relating to Cookery" tr. Barbara Inskip. Maxime Rodinson, A.J. Arberry, Charles Perry, Medieval Arab Cookery: Essays and Translations (Totnes, Devon: Prospect Books, 2006), p. 149.*

Concerning grapes

They are weakly hot and moderately humid and make the body fertile. Even though they produce flatulence during digestion, they are scarcely free of light flatulence in each of the stages of digestion. Harsh and bothersome pains in the belly and the muscles result from them.

Account of its juice

Grape juice is the basis of wines and syrups and vinegars. It is hot and humid. If it is drunk freshly squeezed, it bloats the belly, then causes rumbling noises, and, after two or three days, pains in the organs in most cases, unless its digestion takes place in a strong, young body, and that is rare. But in the majority of cases, this [bloating and pain] will certainly happen.

If it is cooked to a syrup, it is hot and dry and helps digestion and empties the stomach, cleanses the lungs and the bronchi, calms coughing and burning during urination, and is extremely beneficial to the bladder, if it is cooked in clay or copper pots, coated with tin, not stirred while it cooks, but rid of its foam and purified of it with care. After all, those syrups that are modified during cooking will inflame the blood and cause it harm; there is no good in them.

If grape juice is not cooked, it ferments, as is already known, and then it is more harmful than before. If left like that, it becomes forbidden wine. If, before this occurs, one adds vinegar or a solution with a little yeast in it, or a pouring with something acidic in it, such as lime or sour pomegranate juice or the juice of another acidic thing, it becomes vinegar. Vinegar cools and dries. In the same measure as it ages, its dryness increases.

Grapes have been cultivated around the Mediterranean for at least 8,000 years, if not much longer, [4] and they have sparked a whole literary genre in Arabic and Persian—that of wine poetry, or *khamriyyat*.

Their use is described extensively in medieval Arabic cookbooks, with sour grapes being a common souring and preserving agent or used for yogurt-making, but also as the star of the show in meat dishes such as *hisrimiyya* (sour grape stew), made with eggplant and spices or with meatballs, chickpeas, rice, chard, and gourd, as described by Ibn Mubarak Shah. [5]

Sweet grapes seem to have generally been eaten fresh, cooked into syrups to be used in beverages and to sweeten dishes, or preserved to be eaten during the cold season. The *Kitab Wasf al-at'ima al-mu'tada*, an expansion and reworking of the *Kitab al-Tabikh*, mentions a recipe for pickling grapes with vinegar and honey after sealing their stems with wax, [6] while the unknown author of the *Kitab Wusla ila l-habib* claims that "fruit molasses are better" and should be preferred over honey. [7]

While many of these recipes have fallen out of use, figs and grapes continue to enjoy wide popularity. By Ibn Zuhr's lights, both are hot and humid and thus will counterbalance the melancholy that results from an excess of black bile, associated with coldness and dryness. They will instead encourage a sanguine, enthusiastic temperament. However, one should be wary of eating too many dried figs, since their heat and dryness might tip the scales towards a choleric temper. Both figs and grape juice will, at any rate, help digestion—just beware the flatulence!

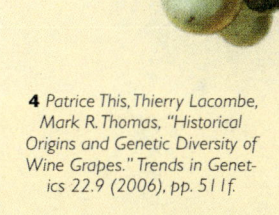

---

[4] Patrice This, Thierry Lacombe, Mark R. Thomas, "Historical Origins and Genetic Diversity of Wine Grapes." Trends in Genetics 22.9 (2006), pp. 511f.

[5] Ibn Mubarak Shah, The Sultan's Feast: A Fifteenth-Century Egyptian Cookbook, tr. Daniel L. Newman (London: Saqi Books, 2020), pp. liv, 36, 45f., 83, 119.

[6] Charles Perry, "The Description of Familiar Foods: Kitab Wasf al-At'ima al-Mu'tada." Maxime Rodinson, A.J. Arberry, Charles Perry, Medieval Arab Cookery: Essays and Translations (Totnes, Devon: Prospect Books, 2006), p. 397.

[7] Anonymous, Scents and Flavors: A Syrian Cookbook, tr. Charles Perry (New York: Library of Arabic Literature, 2020), p. 112.

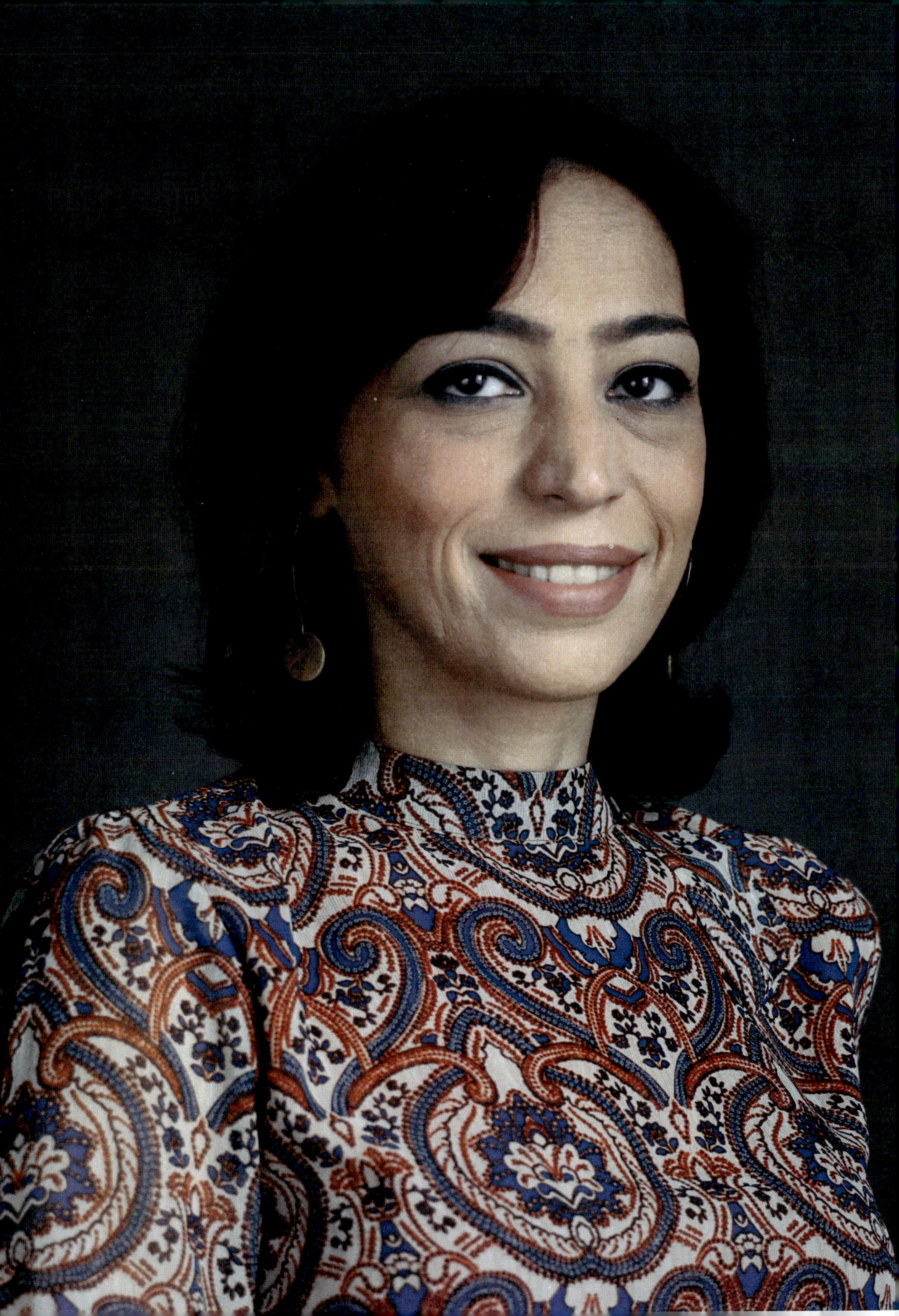

Interview

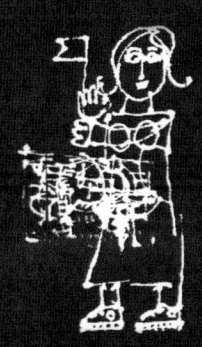

On Fiction's Uneaten Meals

Donia Kamal

By **Asmaa Abdallah**

Photo: Ahmed Abdel Sabour

The first time I read Donia Kamal's *Cigarette Number Seven*, I was in tears. Over the revolution that came to nothing, over the narrator's relationship with her father, over all her other relationships. It stayed with me for years.

The author later said, in an interview, that she'd been overcome by the idea of "unfinished dreams" and built the novel around that, as well as the desire to bring her long-deceased father back to life, so he could experience the revolution.

I read the novel again this year, with a fresh round of tears at all that could have been, but also with a new appreciation of the book's meals: described in detail, yet mostly left uneaten.

Cigarette Number Seven **is filled with food references: long paragraphs of characters examining, buying, and prepping dishes, ingredient by ingredient, then chopping and mixing and cooking. From the chicken-and-potato dish in the first chapter to the homemade fuul and moussaka later on, the reader can almost smell and see these sumptuous meals. Yet there are no descriptions of anyone actually eating or tasting them. The act of consuming is left to the imagination, or the reader is explicitly told that the food went uneaten.**

Donia Kamal: All the details of food prep, and the descriptions of ingredients, were meant to develop the main character, whose character is reflected in her choice of raw vegetables and her method of cooking. Cooking is a central way in which the narrator feels; it reflects her state of mind and how she perceives the events and people around her. So it was more important for me to write about the process of *making* the food rather than about people eating it.

One of the few references to food being consumed is when Nadia eats—well, even smears her face with—the ice cream that her father got her. Does this show us that theirs is the only functioning relationship?

DK: Yes, the relationship between the narrator and her father is the one round, wholesome relationship in the narrative.

In many parts of the book, Nadia cooks for her father or for her boyfriend Ali. The former, we come to learn, has been dead for many years, while she constantly expects the latter to leave.

DK: Some people can only show their love for others by making them food. Nadia is always making food for the people she cares for; this is true with Ali and with the father. As for leaving, it is part of the narrative's dilemma. Parting roads, break-ups, death, and all forms of leaving are the core of the story. Even as the reader gets to know that her father hasn't been physically present, Nadia *makes* him present by describing his favorite meals and the time she spent preparing them. Ali is a different story; Nadia is always comforting him by making him his favorite meals, for instance when they have a fight, or when he ditches her once or twice, and the food is thrown in the trash as a sign of her disappointment in their relationship. Food can be an agent of love and comfort; it can be a sign of failure and sorrow.

The food each character prefers hints at their personality. For Nadia's father, it's traditional Egyptian classics such as fuul, while her boyfriend likes mashed potatoes, and Nadia is happy to make both. When Nadia leaves for the US, will her cooking also adapt to the people she is feeding, or will she want to protect her cooking memories?

DK: This is a question for Part 2 of *Cigarette Number Seven*, if there is such a thing! Since this part hasn't been written, there is no right answer. She may need to satisfy the people around her by learning how to make their favorite meals, and she might try to impress them with her skills in making traditional Egyptian food. We may never know!

Most of the cooking scenes were accompanied by music, which also pervades the novel.

DK: It was very much intentional for those scenes to be touching the readers' senses. Also, don't forget that having a radio in the kitchen is something that exists in the back of the heads of most Egyptian women. This radio might have been in a mother's or a grandmother's kitchen, but it was there. The radio, and some staticky old tunes, are common kitchen memories. I was trying to bring back that memory, to make the scenes real and warm.

As a child, Nadia seems to take more pleasure in *anticipating* food—such as when she's waiting for the colorful bounty of rice, chicken, and potatoes that her grandmother will serve her—while, as an adult, she seems to take more pleasure from *preparing* it.

DK: As a child, her pleasure came from sitting in the kitchen and watching her grandmother prepare everything from scratch until she reached the stage of the fully cooked meal. The pleasure came from the mystery of the process in her young eyes; yes, from the anticipation. As an adult, she recreated the process as she'd seen it when she was young, and so cooking was more of a legacy that related to warmth and love, rather than about consuming food.

Near the end of the novel, as Nadia's relationship and life unravel, we are told of "a smell of decay in the kitchen," for which she can find no source or remedy. It's ironic that this happens in the kitchen and not in another part of her small studio apartment—the couch perhaps, where she spends most of her time, and which she claims is her "ultimate pleasure."

DK: This was the cathartic scene in which Nadia rids herself of all her nightmares and failures. The kitchen was where she cooked her emotions, and so it was the kitchen where these outdated emotions had to be expelled.

Adept as she is in the kitchen, Nadia does not dare make her father's homemade fuul, even though she knows the recipe well. This is understandable, given her grief. Yet she keeps a bag of dried beans in her kitchen at all times. Is there hope that she'll make it one day, perhaps as a sign of making peace with his departure?

DK: This dish was her father's specialty. It contained all the warmth of a safe childhood before everything in Nadia's life went south. This meal was her representation of family and of comfort; it was described as a hardship for Nadia to prepare or recreate the same dish, since she couldn't recreate everything that came with the meal. The beans in her kitchen were only a symbol of what she'd lost and could not bring back, no matter how well she cooked.

There is a green pepper mirroring an eagle on the back cover. How did that come about?

DK: That was the brilliant idea of the artist who designed the cover of the book, Ahmed Al Labbad. He linked the events of the revolution with cooking in the book, and thus came up with this green pepper eagle that you saw on the back cover. I fell in love with the design the minute I saw it.

Which meal in *Cigarette Number Seven* did you most relish portraying?

DK: I loved writing all of them, but the potato-and-chicken meal that the grandmother prepared was a scene I liked writing a lot. But it was the moussaka that got me many comments from readers, who used this part as a recipe.

Do you like fiction that features food and cooking? Does food also take center stage in your other books?

DK: I like writing about anything that touches the senses. For me, this was the first time to write about food; my first novel had zero cooking scenes, and my most recent one is an epistolary novel that also did not include any cooking. I have to say I enjoyed writing the food sections more than I'd expected.

Sheikh Zayed Book Award

جائزة الشيخ زايد للكتاب

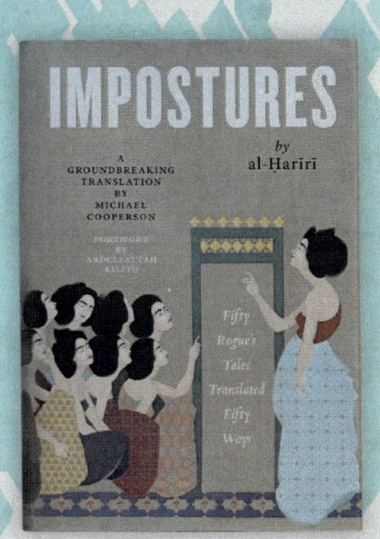

Translation Award Winner

IMPOSTURES BY AL-HARIRI
translated by Michael Cooperson

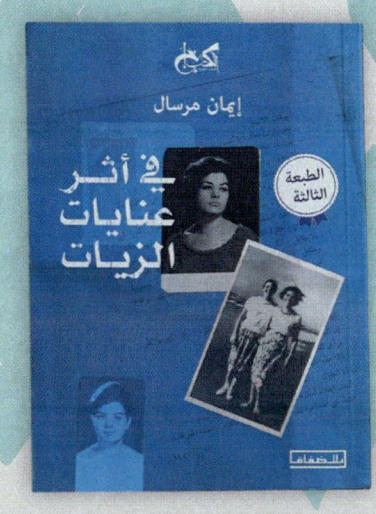

Literature Award Winner

(IN THE FOOTSTEPS OF ENAYAT AL-ZAYYAT)
by Iman Mersal

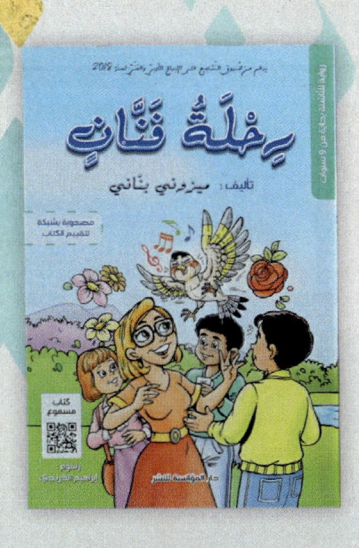

Children's Literature Award Winner

(AN ARTIST'S JOURNEY)
by Mizouni Bannani

CELEBRATING ARAB WRITING

The Sheikh Zayed Book Award has announced the winners of its 15th edition across eight key categories.

Follow the story online…

@zayedbookaward

TRANSLATION GRANT AVAILABLE

Translation Grant is available for winners and shortlisted titles in the Literature and Children's Literature Award. Head to the prize website to find out more about the books and the funding available.

مركز أبوظبي للغة العربية
Abu Dhabi Arabic Language Centre

Discover more at:
zayedaward.ae

Workshop

The Taste of Letters

By **Nour Kamel**

"The Taste of Letters" was a two-month workshop that took place in November and December of 2019 as part of "Botoun," a project focused on the politics and practices of food distribution, production, and consumption at the Contemporary Image Collective (CiC) in Cairo.

The name of the workshop was inspired by a 2017 talk given by the poet Iman Mersal, in which she reflected on the taste of letters in the alphabet soups commonly found in Canadian supermarkets. Mersal wondered what Arabic letters would taste like, were an Arabic alphabet soup to exist. "طعم الحروف" also became the name of the collection of the five following texts, translated here for the first time to English.

Eman Abdelhamid Kamal's poignant "**How I Cook Love in Three Steps**" takes us through a woman's deeply personal journey through the dynamics of love and labor inherent in the act of cooking for others. **Moza Almatrooshi's** "**From Farm to Table**" gives voice to the voiceless—the living organisms that are our food. **Samaa Elturkey's** "**The Loaf of Bread We Broke Together**" is an intimate letter of shared womanhood and healing through the communal act of baking and cooking, and **Rania Hilal's** "**The Meeting Space**" lets us glimpse the wonder, fantasies, and dark corners of one woman's kitchen. Finally, **Amira Mousa's** "**Beyond a Herring Recipe**" neatly ties up this collection of texts, exploring the challenges of writing a personal text about food while reflecting on her relationship to writing.

The idea of a writing workshop centered on our personal relationships to food was originally suggested by writer and translator Mariam Boctor. As we designed the syllabus, along with writer and editor Maie Panaga, we were frustrated by what we found to be a palpable gap in Arabic literature. We're hopeful that this workshop and the texts it helped foster will be a step in expanding the realm of contemporary writing about food in Arabic, particularly by women.

How I Cook Love in Three Steps

By **Eman Abdelhamid Kamal**, translated by **Mariam Boctor**

Today, I have to get up and prepare the usual: love!

It took me a long time to understand that cooking him a meal was one of the few ways I could express love in a form he could receive. And thus, I am obliged to serve it up—like so.

All the possible reasons for remaining exactly as I am race around my head while I lie, motionless, staring at the ceiling. Or curled up in a corner of the couch: as if taking up less space might lessen the pain. The hours drag on, with no answer dense enough to satisfy the hunger called up by the question: Why am I alive today?

An emptiness drags me down, keeping me pinned to the floor. My feet crumble under this heavy presence and cannot stay steady. I introduce the thought repetitively, in order to coax my brain into slowly coming to terms with what's needed: I have to make dinner, I have to cook up some love!

When the thought becomes sufficiently compelling, it takes me to the kitchen. That far-off space, always excessively cold, the opposite of how it should be. My eyes fall on the pile of dishes that occupies the tiny sink, the crumbs of food scattered across the floor, and the garbage can filled to the brim and in need of emptying, cleaning, and airing. Heaviness coalesces into a blur, playing with my vision. It becomes hard to distinguish the color of the wooden furniture, which is my favorite shade of purple. My uncle had insisted that the workers redo it when they failed to get the shade exactly right, even though it cost him extra. This kitchen was his wedding gift to me, and, at the time, I didn't think too much about his choice of gift.

At first, I tried to follow advice from one of my friends, to turn washing the dishes into "a meditative ritual," as she called it. Focus on the details of the drawings and decorative motifs on the different pots and pans. On the feeling of the water flowing over my hands. I would play music, humming along with the wrong words. Now this "ritual" was akin to the hard labor imposed on prisoners. As I'm forced to tackle layer upon layer of congealed fats, destructive thoughts congeal over the surfaces in my head, sealing all the windows. The water is always cold, because the tap's been broken since forever. I have to empty out the lone, small sink so I can rinse the rice and vegetables. I need to make room on the neighboring surface (which is always occupied with various items), for some defrosting meat.

The same place that was a stage for my culinary adventures now reminds me of the straitened dimensions of my existence, with its width that does not exceed roughly a meter and a half. And its height is barely three meters, which has to hold all the appliances, utensils, and pots my mother bought in preparation for my marriage, so she could rest assured that she had fulfilled her maternal duties. I don't remember choosing the plates or the pans; back then, I was fighting other battles. I didn't know I had it in me to care about such details. Now, I know I do. I not only have to concern myself with all these details, but I also must develop a capacity for appreciating them. I can't deny that I have grown fond of certain items: the plates for Chinese noodles, the precision of the coffee cups. But there is an excess of things to choose from, adding to the state of perplexity and even more to the state of congestion.

I pull my mind back from regurgitating all these thoughts, reminding myself of the task at hand. My feet hurt from standing under this miserable weight, and my hands want nothing more than to escape the unbearably sticky dish-soap sensation. Something this heavy cannot be a meditative ritual. I have to wash the rice until the water is translucent, then soak it for at least half an hour. They say this will rid the rice of starchiness. Perhaps I'll defrost the meat in the microwave, as I seem to be running out of time. So the dinner menu for today will be rice, beef, and sauteed vegetables. But stop! He doesn't eat sauteed vegetables, and he doesn't like vegetable salad: a pet peeve carried over from his childhood. What side dish can I serve that conveys nutritional value as well as affection?

This hesitation stirs some pent-up anger, bringing it to the surface. I don't approve of his eating habits and his appetite for everything unhealthy. When I tell him this, he tells me that love is about acceptance. I need not approve of his choices, and it's okay if I don't, but in any event it's no reason to be angry. Deep down I know this to be true, but I can't always find a reason for my perpetually boiling anger.

He tells me that he needs a warm meal every day, a reason to want to come home. Every time we have this conversation, my sobbing gets out of control. I pretend to be strong, to have it all together, taking in deep breaths and exhaling them slowly. But I can't help but break into silent sobs, until I start choking on uncontrollable tears. In that moment, all I want is for everything to stop, for all the sobbing to cease. For the load to become a little lighter. For the river of anger, churning in my chest and threatening to drown me, to let up just a little. Of course, this never happens. I can't just allow myself to cry and leave off our ping-pong game of blame and shame. Each one of us blames the other for the hardship we suffer alone: disappointment for failing to meet the unrealistic expectations we set for one another. He becomes my opponent, and I am swift on the offensive. My guard is always up, to shield me from any impending enemy attacks. But he is not my enemy, far from it!

The uncertainty makes me uncomfortable, and my troubled soul wants nothing more than stillness, as if someone had thrown a rock into my motionless lake. I need a side dish to go with the white rice, something that's not vegetables or a salad. Something soft to coat my hard-hearted, thorny love. He isn't too crazy about red sauce but he likes it with fattah. That inimitable dish—the one people gather around during feasts, which is also prepared during periods of mourning to comfort those who have lost a loved one—is coincidentally one of his favorite foods. His mother recently shared her particular recipe for fattah. Fattah it is then, for today's serving of love.

For now, the creases on my forehead (my face's reaction to an impending migraine) will be set aside along with the pains in my back, which my mother attributes to my laziness and weight gain, and that a book I'm reading explains as a symptom of evading the weight of responsibility. There is no more time for cathartic sobbing, nor for changing the mismatched dreary outfit I've been wearing at home all day. I have to make some love.

I get out beef, around three hundred grams. I cut the meat into medium-sized cubes, taking care to remove all the fatty bits: just the way he likes it. I put a non-stick pan on medium heat. To the pan, I add a spoonful of butter and some oil. As soon as the butter melts, I gently add the pieces of meat, making sure the oil doesn't splatter and burn my hands. A sprinkle of salt and pepper on the upturned side. I wait for three minutes, or maybe five, then flip the meat over and repeat. The noise in my head stops. I watch the meat change color.

When the distinct aroma of meat cooked in butter starts wafting up, I get a clove of garlic and split it vertically, rubbing each half softly against the surface of the chopped meat. I flip the meat and repeat this step on the other side. This imparts a subtle background flavor of garlic, with the flavor of the meat taking center stage. I add a little over two cups of water to the pan and slightly reduce the flame. I add the magic blend needed for a fitting stock: bay leaves, cardamom, a dash of nutmeg, cinnamon.

I cover the pan and leave it.

I turn down the flame. I turn down the intensity of my resentment, the source of which I struggle to identify. The anger building up inside me has become like a dormant volcano, threatening to erupt any day. It coats every feeling moving through me, and drops of molten flame punctuate my every attempt at communication. It inhabits the wrinkles starting to appear around my eyes and mouth, and the lines across the length of my forehead.

It's an anger crouching behind fake acceptance. It occupies the depths of my eyeballs so that, no matter where I look, I cannot see except through its lens. Its internal temperature is constantly rising, although it never loses the solidity of an iceberg. Its heavy ashes are coated with a layer of detestable brown, an anger I try to lose in colors. I deposit it in the meals I make in an attempt to escape it. Or perhaps I lose it in the colorlessness.

I move in the direction of the soaked rice. I pour it in a strainer until the excess water is gone. In a suitable pot, once again, I add a mixture of butter and oil, just enough to coat the grains of rice with a delicate gloss, not a measure more. I deposit the strained rice into the pot and stir the grains gently with a wooden spoon over medium heat for another three minutes. Then I add water, cold or warm, whatever is on hand, until it barely covers the rice. I add some salt, nothing more. I wait until the water starts to boil, then reduce the flame to the lowest possible point and cover the rice. I set the oven timer to twelve minutes. As soon as it goes off, I turn off the flame. I don't uncover the rice until an equivalent amount of time has passed, to allow the grains to expand fully and come to a rest.

So far, nothing particularly special is going on, just beef and rice. Time for the plot twist and the dish's finale! I prepare two loaves of baladi bread, cutting the bread into medium-sized squares. I arrange the squares on an oven tray. I don't like to deep fry it, the way some people do. I prefer the gentle crunch that comes from toasting bread in the oven, and the scent that wafts out. In a small plate I melt some butter, adding a minced clove of garlic, salt, and a pinch of thyme. I baste the bread squares with this paste and then place the tray in the oven for about twenty minutes. I remember how adding garlic to the toasted bread was my first personal twist on the recipe. We end up with bite-sized bread that's taken on a golden-brown color and a palpable crunch.

The tomato sauce is what makes the difference between the fattah my mother makes and the one his mother makes (his favorite). I believe it's what sets each version of fattah apart. I ask him time and again about his opinion on the matter, repeating my question until I get the answer I want to hear. He agrees with me and gives my detailed questions terse responses; he tells me he likes my fattah, yes, otherwise he wouldn't eat it, but my question remains unanswered, waiting for another chance to be asked.

To prepare the tomato sauce, I strain some tomato juice and then heat it on a flame until it acquires a puree-like consistency. To the puree, I add a spoon of canned tomato paste. In a separate pan, once again, I add some minced garlic and oil. As soon as the oil caresses the garlic and their exultant odors waft up, I add some vinegar, the tomato puree, and some of the previously prepared beef stock. As soon as it starts to boil, I add the requisite seasonings: salt, black pepper, cumin, chili powder, and a pinch of thyme. I also add a teaspoon of sugar or honey to balance the acidity of the tomatoes and leave it to boil over medium heat until the sauce acquires the required consistency.

I execute the recipe's final step with the remaining ounces of patience I possess. The soup is to be drizzled over the toasted bread. Some garlic and butter:

as soon as they start to bubble, I add two or more spoonfuls of beef stock and a spoonful of vinegar. Let it all boil, then turn off the flame.

Serving time has come. The time of absolution. The time that's dumped along with everything else into the serving dish, the table left to stutter under its abiding weight. Now the enjoyable part: I can concentrate on the colors, their coordination, and the coming-together of all the different smells. Love in a form that can be swallowed and consumed.

In a rectangular glass serving dish, I arrange the toasted bread, drizzling it with the soup. Then comes the tomato sauce, and finally a layer of white rice for the cubes of meat to frolic on, jewels in a royal crown, and some glistening red tomato sauce here and there to compliment the picture.

I place the serving dish on a small table, adjacent to the unshuttered balcony, which carries the last rays of sunlight inside. I take a picture to document the beginning of the journey and its completion. The picture goes into the gallery on my phone, or maybe a sexy Instagram post.

Then I sink into the nearest chair. And wait.

From Farm to Table

By **Moza Almatrooshi**, translated by the author

On our farm, we take care to harvest only the best of crops. We prioritize divine intervention, in the form of rain, and we minimize our reliance on man-made irrigation.

The sky's back bends and weakens in the face of the rain, which invades the soil, which is already imprisoned by the earth and cannot escape. The rain mobilizes the wind, as well as an army of birds and bees to snatch the seeds from their homes and hurl them far from their origins. The rain then readies itself for colonization, to expand its empire, and digs its sharp daggers into the body of the soil. These stabs melt into the dirt. Then the sun arrives to conquer the rain with its sharp rays. The sun weeps for the fruits born of the illicit relationship between rain and soil. It cares for them from a distance, but it cannot protect them from looming dangers. The soil does not ache when its fruits are pulled out of its bellies. The methods of pulling these fruits are varied, and they pass through hands, fingers, mouths, noses, and beaks. There's also picking, cutting, trampling. Any violence that relieves the soil of the burden of bearing fruit is welcome, regardless of technique, even if it creates scars that don't heal. The fruits are an unintended consequence of the rain's invasion. Eventually, some of them resist these violences and remain on the soil's back, turning into fruit-bearers, and thus again suffering the same fate.

The transition

After the harvest, we check our produce with meticulous attention, and then we make a careful selection based on the look and feel of the fruits' color, texture, size, and shape. At its peak, the produce is transported from the farm to the market. Ready to be in your hands.

Fear hangs over the produce at every gust of wind, no matter how weak, and at the passage of any alien creature, no matter how miniscule. This fear is justified by the atrocities that befall the soil. A great giant with monumental circular arms smacks the produce out of its place, and the abuse by two- and four-legged animals is never-ending, while worms and birds reach even those who seek refuge in the heights. Another giant is loaded up with cells that are filled with fresh prisoners, who cannot imagine where they are about to be taken. Their cries, screams, and calls for help go unheeded, as the giant races the wind on its spinning legs.

The market

You'll find us keen to preserve the freshness of the produce with which we've been entrusted, even after you have selected it at the market.

The produce gets transported from its cells to a vast and boundless space, where there is a blinding light but no sun, a place that's cold and void of nourishment. The fruits are segregated in hilly zones, with no guardians to protect them from the chill air, decay, death, or any other element of time and place. The greatest threats are the palms that snatch those who've managed to survive. The produce then gets placed on a moving path that jettisons them into an open grave. The non-sunlight grows opaque.

The kitchen

We provide a cookbook so we can join you in your kitchen, where we help you select the best way to transform our produce into delicious dishes, satisfying all tastes.

A sense of helplessness might nearly overwhelm the produce, in its fear of this new environment, were it not completely different from the one before it. They had thought they would never see any kind of light again, that their condition would remain just as before. But they soon realize the difference between yesterday's detention and today's: the space is smaller, its heights are equal in length and width, and the sunlight is able to sneak in ever-so-faintly when the false light is relieved of its guard post. It is nearly impossible for them to rejoin the sun, no matter how desperate their need grows. The fruits are led to the insides of yet another giant, tucked into its cold hollows. Unlike the flesh that's stored in there, the produce is still alive. Is this what they will turn into? They are no longer able to identify what is living and what has passed, nor can they remember what they were before the days dragged them to this fate. Their questions stop once the belly of the frosty giant is opened. They are now ready to meet their ends: thrown, flogged, chopped, pressurized, burnt, cursed.

The plate

It is possible to combine our produce with your favorite dishes, or you can come up with an innovative recipe of your very own!

The bodies dance passionately in their fated hell, which comes to them all. The dead flesh mixes with the flesh of the living, and everyone gets a new skin that conceals the old one that once covered them. They move, without resistance, as their souls peel out of their bodies. They are laid out on a myriad of altars, as if prepared as offerings for greedy gods.

The table

Bon appetit!

The stench of bodies means it's time to eat.

The Loaf of Bread We Broke Together

By **Samaa Elturkey**, translated by **Mariam Boctor**

My Dearest A,

I hope you're doing well. I've been thinking about you ever since the last time we met, in the parlor of al-Dhaher House. We were beneath the stained-glass windows, and the sunlight poured in between the colors, creating a game board for our lazy imaginations. We couldn't distinguish the golden yellow of the sunlight from the colors of the glass, covered as it was with a thick grey dust—the dust no Cairene can elude, the dust you were never able to get used to. The remnants of these patterns on the tiles were choked with too many memories, and none of the original colors showed through. The image I have of that day is an amalgam of colors, memories, lights, and smells that have accumulated and bleed slowly into one another. Each part has its own distinct texture, smell, and tone. But they all come together to form one composite scene.

Yesterday, I received the letter you sent in response to my basket of bread. I know very well that I sent only half-loaves, and I also know that we spent a long time together: baking, kneading, waiting, and fermenting until your fingers went numb. So why, after all this effort, did you only get half-loaves? In this letter, I'll tell you my first story, the one that began before the birth of the early morning hours of Al Dhuha. [1] When the petals of the sun had not yet found a center to revolve around. When we were all unborn. Microscopic in the womb of one Great Mother. My story starts on the day we first met: when we remembered each other's souls before our bodies ever did. We had this feeling right at the center of our bellies: we were destined for subjugation. We knew that, when the time came for us to leave the womb, umbilical cord attached, we must not cut it. A long time ago, before we began to count and number days, you and I swam in the blood of one Great Mother.

She is the first mother, who held us before we were born as individuals, from the wombs of our biological mothers. We swam as a tribe, and what coursed through your blood coursed through mine. What I have now inherited in my body I had before exchanged with you. The covenant was that the Great Mother would pluck the images, words, and details from our memory, but would leave us with a heart that could find love without a compass. That was her commandment: follow your heart, it knows. And when she left us to the world, each one of us landed in a womb as a transitory phase. The umbilical cord, she left between us. Inevitably, we found each other. These are the ties of the first mother and the magic of kin. We were destined to meet. When we were cursed, in the land, we pushed past the crowds to find our place and recognize our kind. And when we saw them, we fell instantly in love. Our visual memories were erased, and our brain cells were unable to conjure where and when we'd met before. But in our guts we knew. The instinct that was located in the center of our bellies—it knew.

We were born in different cities, connected only by winding desert roads. It took more than twenty years for us to arrive, and here we are. I remember falling in love with you at first sight. I felt a tingle in my umbilical cord, a pulse in the center of my belly. Something told me that behind your eyes, you knew me like I knew you. When you fell on the stairs that day, my knee bruised blue. And when you laid sobbing on the couch, I tasted the saltiness of tears in my throat. Life propels you, and my shoulders move. The movement of my hair turns the fan in your room around and around and around. The fan that, most days, leaves you cold.

Usually, the invitation to cook together signifies a shared affection. When you feed someone, you warm their bellies, you share love and warmth. This is what the world is desperate to exchange. But what we agreed on was different. You placed your palm

[1] *In Arabic the dhuha literally translates to the morning/dawn hour. It is also one of the titles of a Sura in the Qur'an and can also be taken to mean the first word or the dawn of language.*

on my heart one night and whispered, "Let me share your load, clearing the path between the roads of your frazzled memory." Maybe you're wondering what this has to do with the shared loaves of bread. Let me explain. While we were kneading the dough, you failed to notice the strands of my hair that fell into it, dyeing it gold. And also the magic that dropped from your eyes into the yeast, turning the pound of flour into twenty pounds of fermented dough. While we were preparing the ingredients, I slipped in my history of scrawny thighs and the hormonal tests my mother nagged me to undergo to confirm my femininity. You mixed that with warm water, your heart, your stories I didn't know, the memory of your body and a dozen violences. I received them from you lovingly, with all the affection that could fill a hundred and fifty mornings of baking. And so we share the nights' heaviness: you empty your insides, and I empty all that I'd hid under the linen in my top closet drawer. We carry it all together.

When I was looking for a bread recipe, the chef warned me not to cook with anger or sadness, lest they make their way into the blood of those who would eat my food. Food is broken down after it's digested and makes its way into bones, flesh, and skin. It will imbue the eaters' bodies with an unpeelable sadness. Even if a surgeon were to intervene and excise the tissues dyed with grief, the mourning would not end. As for us, we rush to be dyed with each others' colors. We swallow the pain with a glad acceptance. We don't protest the marks that appear on our bodies, that carry colors that were not ours. The umbilical cord, and the blood we breathed in together, compels me to consume kilograms of your pain. So that your back doesn't break from the weight of stories, sadnessess, pride, guilt, and love tethered to your back: from your clavicle down each vertebrae of your spine.

To knead is to be constant until all the ingredients combine. Do not stop until every atom has changed from its first state. We knead until the dough holds together: the fine flour particles that move like a breeze, and the water that flows like your morning smile, becoming a solid lump. The leavening, which is a theoretically frightening bacterial addition, changes the solid dough into an airy ball. All the ingredients blend, transform, and change as if born anew. We knead until only a few centimetres of the bowl remain untouched by our fingers.

To knead is to move every single part of the back. The sequence begins with gathering the dough in both hands. We lift it high and anchor our motion in the waist and the midpoint of the spine. Stretch, pull, and lower yourself back to the starting point. The act of kneading reminds me of the scene of women in the graveyard, the scene of wailing or lamenting the dead. They gather the dust in both hands, raise it high above their heads, then scatter it back onto the ground. Like some kind of dance, there's a rhythm to it. Gather the dough and raise both of your arms, feel the weight of gravity pulling you toward the ground, and feel the heaviness of carrying your burdens in the lower part of your back. Drop it again and repeat until the dough holds together. Until the sadness ferments, and our grief is blended together, just like a dance.

The kneading has exhausted you. The tips of your fingers have turned blue, and your arms have failed you. You dislocated your shoulder while offloading our stories and last night's tears into the dough. You hurt even as your eyelids drooped with sleep. Worry not, my beloved, the pain will subside in a little while. But I can't promise the tiredness will go away. It's always there. But what I promise is that it will seem a bit lighter if I stretch my arms, wrench off a huge chunk of it, and bury it under my skin. Perhaps I'll attach it to the back of my arm—it will look prettier there. Lay your hands down and let me swallow some of the dregs of what happened yesterday. I can't end the sadness. I can't fix you. I can't live your life for you. I am completely powerless to do that. But I can be real with you. I can tell you I'm in chains. This honesty is what I can give you. I can also anchor my shoulder to your bones, to hold them in place and stop your back from bending any further.

Lay down your hands and wait. The dough can't be baked before it's rested from all the charges it picked up during kneading. It must take its time to ferment and form. It must take its time in silence. And so must you. Allow yourself some stillness. When you are still, all things revolve around you instead of you going around them. You are centered right in the middle, and become the focal point of the sun's orbit instead of losing your breath in the maddening motions of oppression. The world is constantly pushing us to run, that's the trick. It throws one ball at you, then two, then three and more, like a clown in the circus. You are asked to keep the balls in the air, never once dropping a single one. As soon as you start to get the hang of it, more balls are thrown at you, until you get tired and your arms collapse. Then they call you weak. Useless.

Refusal itself becomes an act of resistance. We women inherited dry and miserable loaves from our first mothers. From the womb of my original mother, I learned to look at myself with loathing. So lay down your hands, my beloved. We have nothing to prove. Let the world miss its chance to celebrate our weakness. We are as we wish to be, not as he wishes us to be. And he's definetely a "he"—the first man who kneaded shame into our bread and force-fed it to our mother. From that day forward, the pleasures of women were colored with subjugation.

When you fell asleep yesterday, I finished the final step in the baking process. I rotated the dough, using circular motions, making sure not to pinch it like a juggling clown. Slowly, gently. I don't want to fall into that trap again. I don't want to leave any trace of the clown seeking applause in the folds of the dough. Still, I might have accidentally left some. Please forgive me for that. I took out a jar I'd kept hidden in the pantry for a while. I sprinkled some of the seeds from that plant you gave me last month. I'd named the plant Eshareya, [2] and I put in just enough of the seeds to give the bread a higher nutritional value. I know you're obsessed with that stuff—and it's okay, that side of you makes me chuckle. When I taste food, I head out on a journey of breaking down flavors, textures, and smells, while you break it down into calories, fats, and nutritional value. All right, all right, let's not get into the dangers of obesity right now. I know this topic ticks you off.

When I was done baking, I split each loaf of bread into two equal halves. This way, I can carry under my skin half your stories, your sadnessses, a look of excitement, and a pirouette. And you can carry half of my secrets, battles, and exhaustion. Every loaf we share becomes flesh, blood, and color on my skin. Everything I carried with you, and you with me, becomes a mark on the map of our bodies. You will never get a complete loaf of bread from me. The rest of your loaf is now a wahma on my belly, a mark of craving and the locus of my feelings and my love. [3]

The smells from yesterday's baking still fill the living room. The sun's rays sway in their final dance before sunset, their playful movements reflected in the colors of the window, right above the couch that still carries the smell of your hair and a few breadcrumbs. I hope you aren't still upset about the missing halves. I hope the wahma mark on your belly has grown darker after digesting the halves I sent you. Perhaps you could send me a picture of it? It would be lovely if I hung it next to the kitchen sink. Think about it and let me know?

---

[2] *Eshareya* means one who readily becomes an intimate companion.

[3] *Wahma* is the Arabic for birthmark. The word comes from *waham* which means to crave. In Egyptian folk culture, the wahma appears on the skin of the newborn in the shape of whatever food the pregnant mother had been covertly craving during her pregnancy.

I have loved you since eternity. I patch up my arms
with the traces of your memory.

With love,
Samaa
El Dhaher, Cairo

P.S.: I know you won't remember the recipe after a
few days, so here it is once again:

- a bowl twice the size of your heart
- the ashes of 4 powerful women warriors
- 1 antidepressant tablet crushed into a powder
- 4 tablespoons of pure love (or you can substitute six strong beats of your heart)
- leaven with long nights spent together
- snippets of our histories (for decoration)
- helplessness, all the helplessness you can find
- 4 cm skin from my belly for kneading
- the seeds of familiarity that sprouted in my window last month
- 3 strands of my hair to impart a golden hue
- a generous amount of your magic

The Meeting Space

By **Rania Hilal**, translated by **Elissa Dallimore**

The meeting ground never changes: it is always the kitchen. This beautiful space, where I got used to meeting myself without any airs, and where I meet my other selves just as I love to see them. I melt my fears with a piece of butter on the face of the soup and spread my anger on the marble table, which is why the chopped vegetable cubes are so carefully formed.

In this precious space, before I receive its recurring gifts, I must first give. Otherwise, how can I expect all that is fond and delicious to come from it, when it is sad, dull, and pale, without interest or love? Do I call it "the factory of joy" or "meeting space" or "vast expanse of colors"? I don't know; I will think and may come upon an answer.

I may wake tomorrow morning and go shopping just for the kitchen. I will search for a hollowed-out circle of wood with a thousand garlic blossoms encircling it to hang on the front window for the neighbors. It will drive away the evil spirits and emotions that slip in from time to time, the ones that never leave me to enjoy a moment's satisfaction—I will not exaggerate and say "inner peace," which is in any case impossible. Rather, I look forward to some of the pleasure that I get from my dishes while a part of me gets lost in and blends with them.

I will head to the department of happy wishes and search for a dream-catcher with blue in it; the master of this domain. I will hang it high, over the entrance, for dreams are what inspire new dishes and, when they deem me worthy, rouse recipes from ancient societies carrying information and glimpses from the lives of others, unmarred by conflicts or ambitions.

I will not forget to purchase a big package of butterflies and bows. I will scatter them in the kitchen corners and around my ethereal fridge mirror. The largest share will be next to and around the utensils, plates, and cutlery. As they are scattered, audibly glimmering every few minutes, the utensils will welcome the food in renewed delight and laughter.

When the time comes to cook, I feel zeal mixed with tension, like the feeling children have when their eyes fix on an amusement park for the first time. I anticipate and prepare as if I am going on a journey. The questions multiply inside me: What is the best degree for roasting? Will its color be lively? I draw up a clear plan. My conviction is firm: no dish resembles another, even if its ingredients and methods match. I am never the same person, nor is the air, the weather, and other elements of my ever-changing circumstances.

The palms of my grandmother's hands are the heroes of this space. They are the maestros of all the symphonies playing in the background for every battle, which begins and ends here. Sugar—and perhaps a unique type of salt—are scattered by her palms without ever leaving a noticeable trace. These are the makings of ideal cooking. I will temporarily replace my palm with hers, for she is the most capable and wise with regards to kneading, cooking, and gentle patting. And so the tension and trembling of my hands will vanish, and they can reclaim their stolen peace.

"Qurs filahi," a soft rustic biscuit made with milk and butter, is my mother's most important dish. It will be in the pantry for harsh days full of hopelessness and disappointment. It is best at the beginning or end of one of these days, along with a cup of milky tea. Adding exceptional peace, it works like a drug permeating me slowly; I feel every particle bowing down in tranquility and resignation. I have probably had enough of contemplating the ceiling, enjoying the buzzing that occupies my ear and gradually transforms into a tickling sensation that deliciously spreads all over my body.

I wish the kitchen spirits would flow in to wake me and tickle my nose. Before I even open my eyes in the morning, the smell of rain alternating with vanilla and cinnamon does the trick. There are no stimulants needed to wake me, nor sleeping pills to sedate me—only smells.

The music will cradle me: "Scheherazade" by Korsakov will flow from my favorite space every day, leading with happiness and lightness. If I prepared the Duck a l'Orange or a tajine of pigeon with freekeh, Mozart would amuse me with all his pieces. If I gave my day to kneading or baking, then the notes of his music would ascend and descend and sway with great elegance, just as my fingers move through the dough, making it yield obediently in a charming dance. There is trilece, the Turkish dessert that I dearly love, which may sway with me during Frank Sinatra or Celine Dion. When I get to the stage of mixing the cream with caramel, I will whisper:

> "Like a lazy ocean hugs the shore, hold me close, sway me more"

To be repeated over and over until we are done with each other.

When I finish the trilece and put it in the fridge, I look at myself in the small mirror adorned with black-pepper seeds in the middle of the fridge before I leave to wash off the cream and caramel residue. I whisper one more time along to the song, and Frank's voice will ring out a little more to me and me only:

> "Dear, but my eyes will see only you
> Only you have that magic technique."

From behind the wall of the kitchen, half a small face peeks out at me, and the voice of Yousef, with his blue jumper and shining brown hair, comes to me every fifteen minutes saying, "Mama, I love you." I choose a day or two to allow Adam to scatter his planets and extinct animals over my kitchen table, leaving them free to roam and discover the landscape of our planet. I let him serve them a green salad and instruct them on how to eat it with chopsticks without complaining about the veggie waste scattered here and there.

I will add a small nook at the end of the kitchen or perhaps directly in front of it. I will place a rug decorated with stars, moons, suns, and small pampered animals, and we can dance in front of it whenever we finish a new dish. The dance begins just as the dish leaves from the oven for the world, met with a grand parade befitting a new baby who is looking at the world for the first time through us. It finds a random, dancing world, full of craziness and absurdity.

I am intent on not leaving the market without bundles of appreciation, gratitude, and nostalgia. They will accompany the utensils; neither a plate nor a spoon will go out without carrying one. As each person touches the plate or spoon, they must choose two of these virtues for each meal and add them to their conversation. I will assign the dinner candles to monitor the situation closely. Whenever someone adds a virtue to their conversation, just as salt and pepper are added to their food, all the candles will let loose showers of light, music, and spirits, which will surround the table and cover those present with warmth and affection.

Every Thursday, I will invite a few guests. I may conjure up my favorite space for them, which they can play in. I will invite them to share their secret recipes. I may leave altogether and see how they interact with the space, confide in my dishes, and dance with my favorite spirits. I want to watch their special dances when they finish preparing food. Will they scatter cinnamon or other ingredients that inspire them?

My cousin Heba will be one of the first invited on those Thursdays. She will free herself of her burdens before visiting, leaving her children somewhere safe. She will reclaim her now long-lost childhood for a long-overdue meeting. Rihab, my sister, will come on the second Thursday. She will come to me in a long, silver gown as a fairytale queen, and her black hair will hang down over her shoulders and amplify her height, beauty, and childish, pale features that have been forever striving for mature womanhood. Shaima, my friend, will seem more beautiful without her old glasses, and I anticipate both hummus and tabbouleh from her. She will come, and after her Ayat, another friend whose food I have never tasted. I will invite her to prepare a whole table spread of her choosing. They will come consecutively, as they are closest to me despite the distance.

I will wait for them while I pamper myself with coconut oil on my body in front of the mirror, just before starting one of my favorite movies. It is my belief that their touches will have colors and spirits that will surprise me. Of course, I may be worried about the small things, like the glass plates and the wooden utensils, six bird cups with colors overlapping on the glass, and the tagine that was a gift from my friend's mother, Radwa. I imagine their alarm when dealing with them, for it is necessary to be gentle, to speak in a low voice, and to have a smile the color of the sea on a calm, clear day so that they can better understand them and me.

This Thursday will be an exception: I will invite them all together to share my joy. I will invite Little Red Riding Hood to join me in making apple pie and gingerbread (to help me quiet the ginger). When I decide to make the ice cream, I will invite Snow White and Cinderella. Both of them lived for a time among the forests and experienced nature's spirits where there are snow, roses, and trees, which is precisely what I want for the flavors of my special ice cream. Before we begin devouring our peculiar dinner, I will surprise them by inviting all of their enemies, so that the sky's gray clouds dissipate. The Big Bad Wolf, the vain queen, greedy Gretel, and even the evil witch will all eat together at one table that our hands furnished. Their hearts will be colored with shades of green, and the grey will vanish. We'll see their eyes overflow with tears of yearning and appreciation, dropping from our pores, and into some of our food as we prepare it.

This will be a good end to the weekend. When our evening winds down, and our laughter disappears until next week, I may lie down to sleep, for the day has been kindhearted. My heart will plunge quickly into sleep, chanting across every pulse, "no sorrow after today... no sorrow after today... no sorrow after today."

Help Rebuild Bookstores in Gaza

Samir Mansour Bookshop held more than 100,000 books. Its affiliated publishing house published work by more than 100 writers, including *ArabLit* contributor Hedaya Shamun. Last month, during Israel's relentless aerial assault on Gaza, Israeli forces bombed the Samir Mansour Bookshop to rubble, destroying everything inside. The same day, Gaza's Iqra'a Bookshop was also destroyed.

Support GoFundMe campaigns set up by human rights lawyers, in cooperation with the store owners, to rebuild these essential spaces.

Beyond A Herring Recipe

By **Amira Mousa**, translated by **Mahitab Mahmoud**

I walk in the door of my apartment and head to the kitchen. I throw the herring into a silver pan over roaring flames that tear at its body. I stand at the sink, washing the ideal herring companion: vegetables. The red tomatoes are mixed with green chili peppers and onions. I add vinegar, lemons, cumin, salt, and tahini to the mix, which is now ready for the herring and wheat-bran bread. As for me, I'm ready for an affordable portion of happiness that is exclusively mine to indulge, which I do with unparalleled tenacity.

The excerpt above is from the Ta'm Al-Horouf ("Taste of Letters") Workshop. I wrote it at the beginning of December 2019, and, during the editing process, the workshop editor said, "This is a dish for groups, not individuals. Yet it's different with you; you prepare it for yourself, and you eat it alone." Her comment struck me. It felt as though I'd been attacked. My reply stuck in my throat, and I didn't throw it in her face. It lingered, and so did I. I admit that her response hurt me, not because it was generally hurtful, but because of the realization it birthed, which grew deeper day after day. I prepare the herring dish, and I eat it alone because I am alone. At some point, this was my choice. Yet the price I pay gets fiercer with time.

Loneliness didn't put an end to my selectivity. It didn't stop me from keeping closeness conditioned, relative, demanding, simple, and quiet to the point sometimes of silence. Terms and conditions apply, with the aim of establishing lighter relationships in which no one says or does something because they have to, or to show politeness, but only out of interest. I described this emotional effect of the editor's comment in three paragraphs, and then I stopped jotting down ideas. I had not finished writing.

A few days later, after the editor had read the three paragraphs I wrote because of her comment, she asked: "Why didn't you write about the reasons you eat herring from the very beginning?"

The question was preceded by a writing that took place deep inside of me, as well as what took place beyond eating the herring, and this triggered an inner debate between my selves. I began by contemplating how some of us practice writing as a kind of trick. In an interview I did with a writer who uses his texts as a way of hiding, he explained how he fools those who judge his writing, how he stays protected by his readiness to reply: "I am not my text." But what does he mean? And is this the motive that truly drives me to write?

My house is full of piles of papers and texts: some are mine, and the rest are other people's. Mine are notes, to-do lists, diets, literary reflections, quotes, and notes on various patterns. By coincidence, I discover my texts are similar to those in journal and diary writings. Here, it's not a question of writing, but of sharing and publishing.

I keep thinking about the future, and of the consequences of publishing a text, as if it were never an option, even though I'm the one others share their stories with, and I pass some of those stories on. Am I ready to share a personal text about myself? Am I ready to forego the role of storyteller, where I identify with others' stories, ideas, sources, and styles of narration? This text will make me spare my usual starting points as a journalist, narrator, and researcher. It will relocate me to a new dimension where the narrative is mine in a way that's *crystal clear*.

"The worst thing for a journalist is to become the story," a journalist said at a training workshop I attended a few years ago. Silently, I responded—I'd settled the matter of texts' autonomy and impartiality a while back. I shot down the idea of an objective text, no matter its field of knowledge. To put it simply, we *are* the texts we write. Yet I'd somehow repudiated whatever did not fall under the title of journalism.

I sided with the profession at the expense of my self, or so I claim, as if I'd entered into a legally binding contract without telling anyone, myself included. I've written about myself before, but the new version of me is different; I am more sage, cognizant, and insightful than before, which makes me at times grateful and at times sorry, because awareness hurts, and insight leads us into situations that we would not choose for ourselves. Still, it's okay. By virtue of the novelty of this version of the text, it shall unravel dark sides.

I usually choose who to share my dark side with, and publication will stand between me and my freedom of choice. This might be easier if we didn't place my selectivity, in my fear of publishing, into the context of a selectivity at all times. That includes the best moments, the ones that should logically require me to abandon what brings me only an undesired loneliness. I fly in the face of logic out of knowledge rather than obstinacy.

The text will change from a personal draft, which only I own, and only I know its background (including what has not been written), into a text that belongs to anyone who reads, shares, and discusses it. Publishing exposes the text to autopsy and makes the author subject to ridicule, praise, and learning. Readers examine the writer, investigate their personal background, and put them under their own microscopes, their own systems of evaluation.

Beyond that, something tells me I am not important enough to publicize myself, especially if I self-publish; voices tell me that I am younger, less accomplished; that I have had smoother experiences, a smile that is not lilywhite, a pain that is not too bleak. Echoes arise from being raised to be an ideal person through less-than-ideal methods; from a profession I love that does not acknowledge my existence; from professors and managers whose production registers do not fill my needs; from friends and acquaintances whose narratives exclude my perspective; for those for whom I fight villains, which get defeated by the latter, crushing my dreams in the process; from the priorities of a struggle that dismisses my rights; and from myself for all the times I believed I did not deserve it. As Mahmoud Darwish wrote, "Who am I to say to you what I say to you?"

I find myself both self-transcendent and afraid of writing personal texts. That is how I write sometimes, and how I'm unable to write at others. I fear the text and its absence. In Gloria Anzaldúa's words, "I write because I'm scared of writing, but I'm more scared of not writing." In the beginning, I planned to write about herring as an outcome of a workshop that tackled our personal relationship with food. I firmly chose the form of the text and its content, and I said it was a "light text."

On an evening that followed, I was invaded by long-dormant thoughts and feelings: deep layers of memory, fears, remains, and rubble inside of me. I tried to deal with them on my own. I avoided approaching them except when writing personal texts in hidden files, and in rare conversations with a few people who were very close to me. Despite the permanent presence of those thoughts and feelings, they are not a shareable topic. If I had the chance to write and publish, I would establish a truthful, yet amputated, structure. Since I am one part of a whole world that revolves around an orbit and yet does not penetrate it, I decided to write about herring. The faith in writing as an act of unearthing rather than constructing, however, demolished the structure; it trespassed on my amputated truthfulness. What is dormant in me decided to rebel against me, and it decided to reveal itself, regardless of the destiny of the text.

All right—this text is not the sort that would make a person's tears fall onto their plate of herring. It's a light text that is, in the end, not about herring. It's about the desire to ignore what lies beyond the words: a partitioned reality that does not embrace my fears and pain.

Dictionary

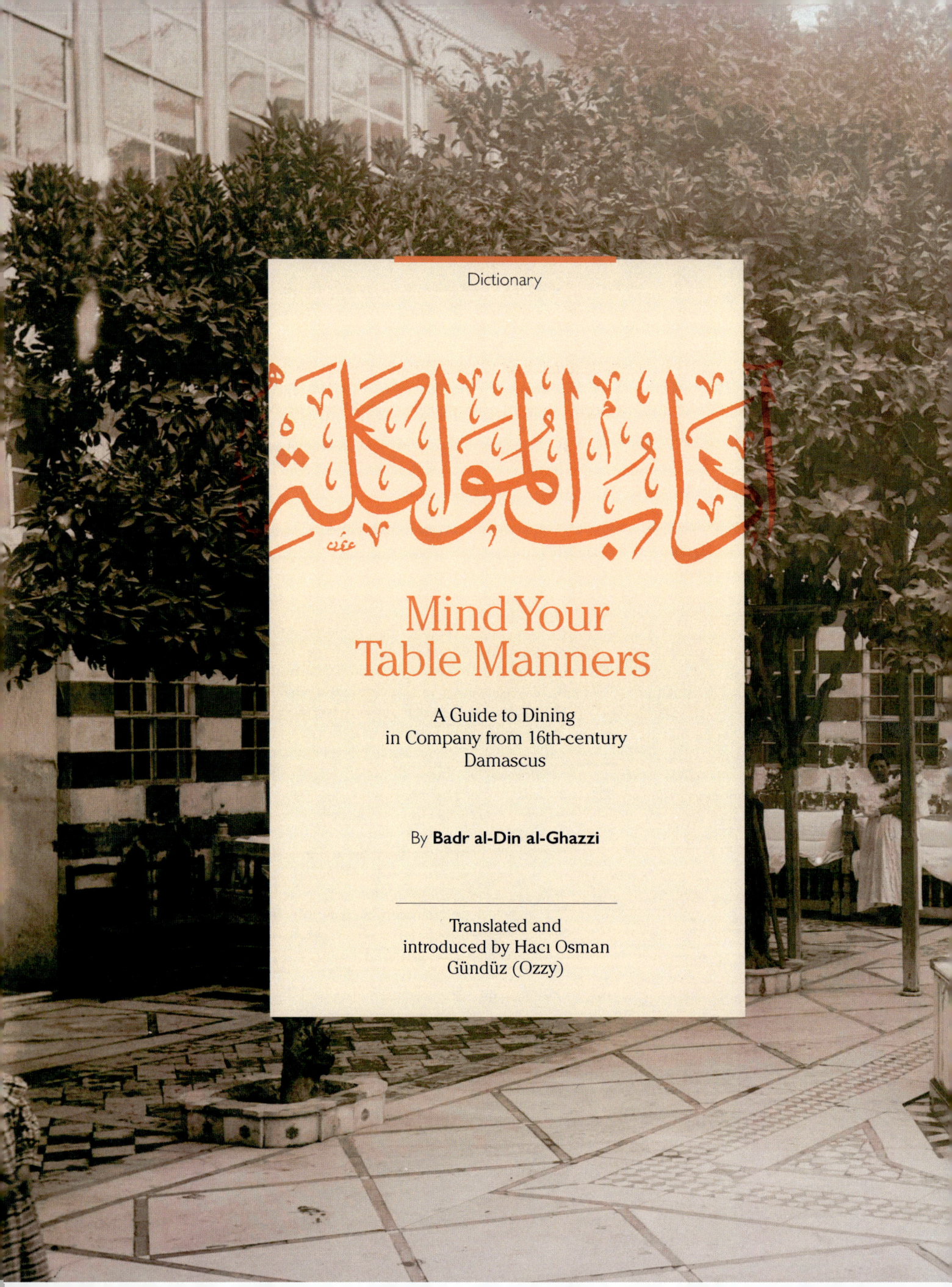

آداب المواكلة

Mind Your Table Manners

A Guide to Dining in Company from 16th-century Damascus

By **Badr al-Din al-Ghazzi**

Translated and introduced by Hacı Osman Gündüz (Ozzy)

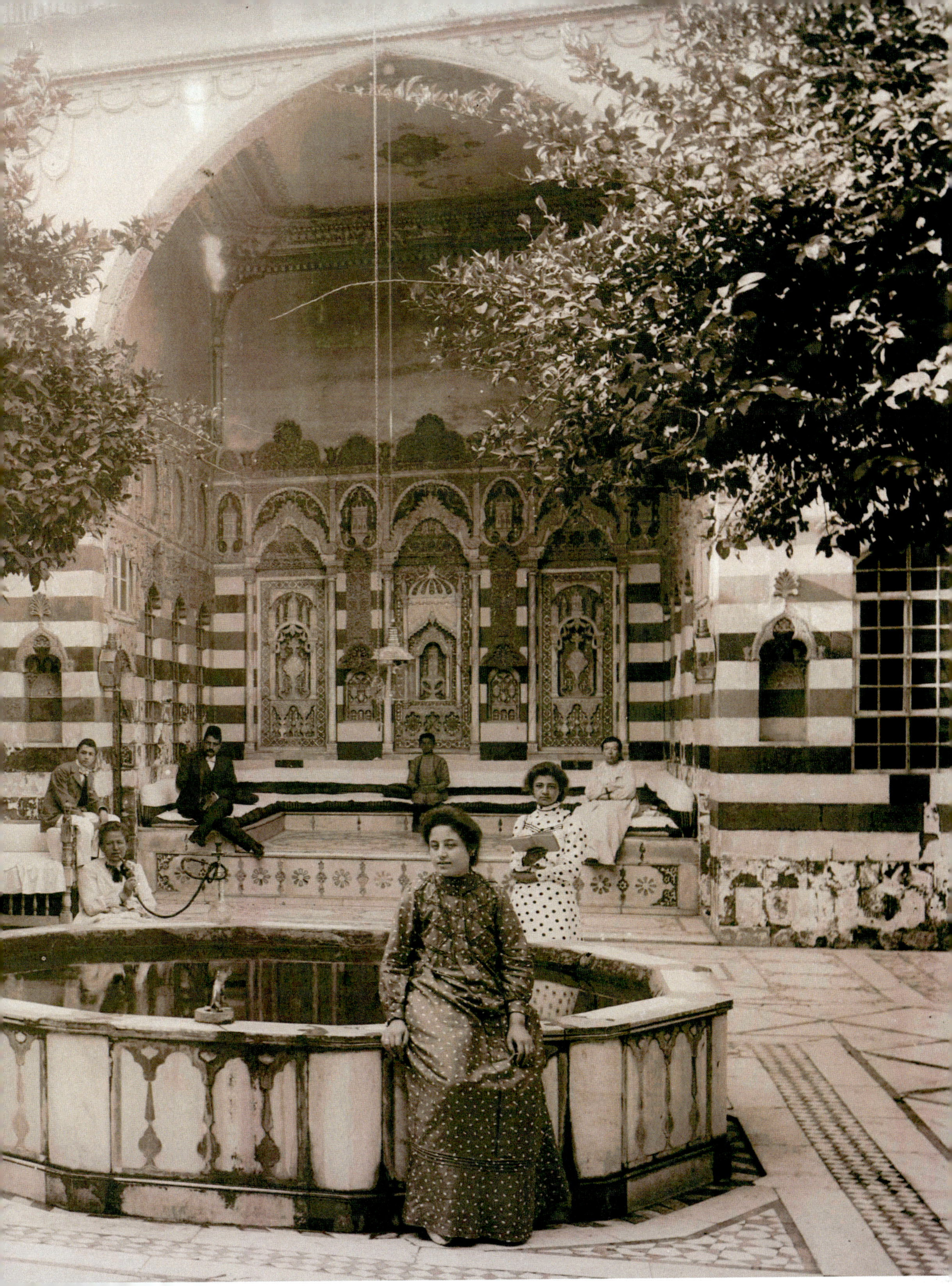

Ottoman-era Damascene scholar **Badr al-Din al-Ghazzi**'s (d. 1577) impressive scholarship covers Islamic law (*fiqh*), Quranic exegesis (*tafsir*), travel accounts (*rihlah*), and poetry, as well as table manners. His treatise, "*Adab al-mu'akalah* (Etiquette of Social Dining)," is a list of defects and shortcomings one needed to avoid, as a guest and a host, to be a respected member of society. This short, dictionary-like collection brings together eighty-one unmannerly shortcomings with definitions that include prophetic traditions, amusing anecdotes, and excerpts of poetry.

The treatise belongs to the personal library of 'Umar Musa Basha (d. 2016), a prolific scholar of the so-called decline period of Arabic literature (1258-1789). Basha edited and published the treatise for the first time in the *Journal of the Arab Academy* of Damascus in 1967.[1] The work was published as a separate booklet by the journal in the same year.[2] It was republished in 1987 with a new introduction by the author.[3] I have based my translation of twenty entries on the 1987 edition.

Among those al-Ghazzi admonishes are people who are late to a dinner party, those who drive others mad with their loud chewing, and people who lick their fingers and continue to eat. The latter faux pas may not raise red flags with contemporary eaters, but this was a period when people often ate from communal plates. Licking fingers, scratching body parts, and handling unsanitary objects were all definite no-nos.

[1] 'Umar Musa Basha, "Risalat adab al-mu'akalah li-l-shaykh Badr al-Din Muhammad al-Ghazzi," *Majallat Majma' al-Lugha al-'Arabiyya bi-Dimashq*, 42 (1967), 503-524 and 732-757.

[2] Badr al-Din Muhammad al-Ghazzi, *Risalat adab al-mu'akalah*, ed. 'Umar Musa Basha (Damascus: Matbu'at Majma' al-Lugha al-'Arabiyya bi-Dimashq, 1967).

[3] Badr al-Din Muhammad al-Ghazzi, *Risalat adab al-mu'akalah*, ed. 'Umar Musa Basha (Damascus and Beirut: Dar Ibn Kathir, 1987).

Previous spread
**Court of a Damascus home
ca. 1890**
Library of Congress

Listen to an audio feature from The Metropolitan

Following pages
Damascus Room
A residential reception chamber (qa'a) typical of the late Ottoman period in Damascus, Syria. Among the earliest extant, nearly complete interiors of its kind, the room's large scale and refined decoration suggest that it was part of the house of an important, affluent family. Poetry inscribed on its walls indicates that the patron was Muslim and possibly a member of the religious elite who were believed to have descended from the Prophet Muhammad.

© The MET

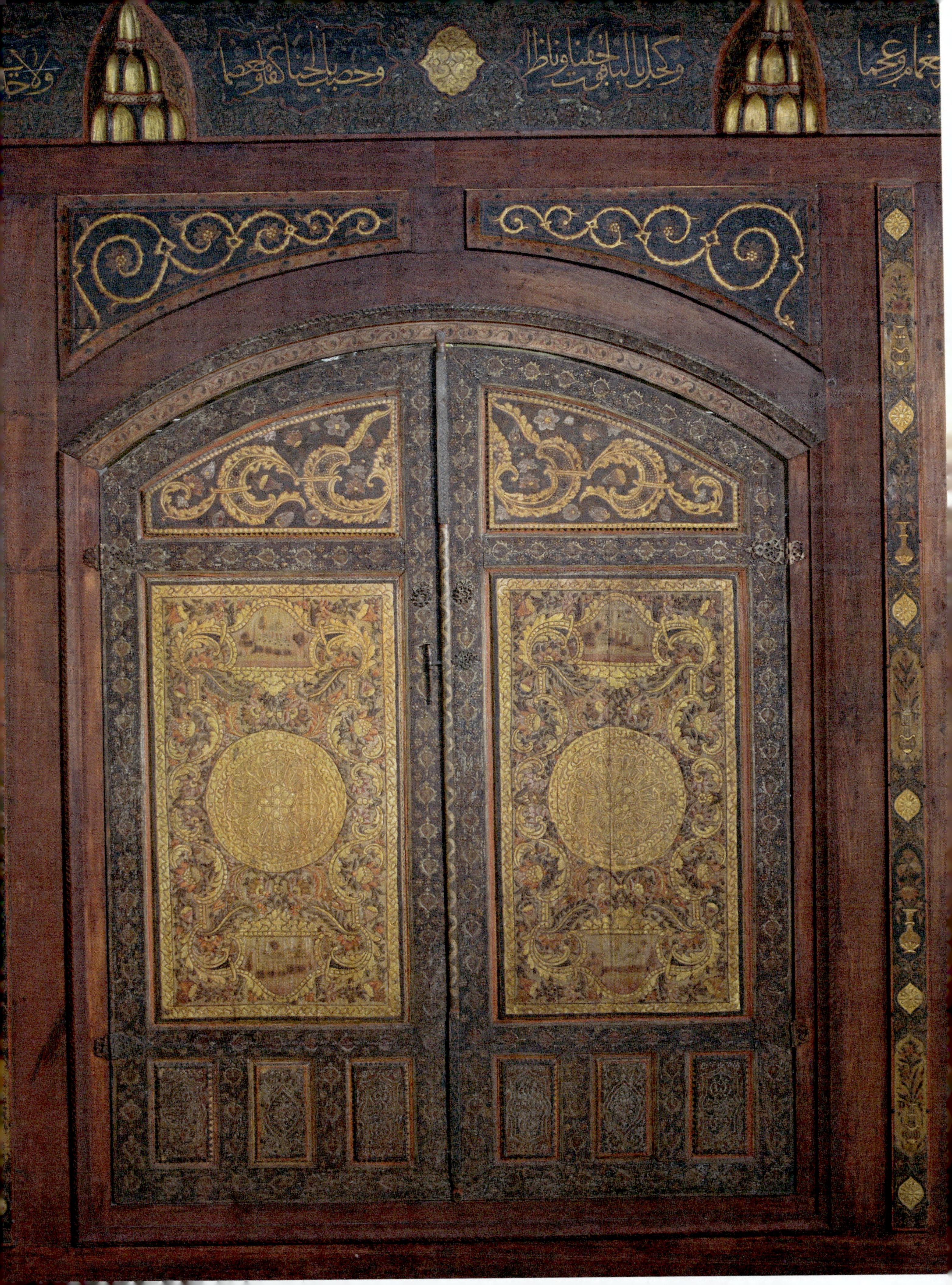

In the Name of God, the Beneficent and the Merciful

Praise is due to God, and greetings upon His chosen servants. This is a list of shortcomings, and whoever knows them well becomes an expert in the etiquette of social dining. There are eighty-one shortcomings, and we have presented each separately. God is He who gives success. Here they are:

The Crawler (*al-zahif*)

The crawler is one who, when food is served, crawls onto the table before others, heedless of the fact that the food may not have been fully laid out or that the host may be waiting for the arrival of other expected guests. If the others approach the table just as he does, he voraciously serves himself double. If the others take their time in joining him, he remains at the table alone in shame. Perhaps the food was intended for someone the host was expecting. That the crawler rushes into eating before others is an unpleasant burden on the host.

The Dilatory (*al-mutathaqil*)

A dilatory fellow is one who gets invited to a meal and accepts the invitation. People trust he will honor his word, but he keeps the anxious host waiting, thus starving and tormenting the host and other guests. The best way of dealing with this, after finding out what his excuses are and sending back the messenger, is for others to go ahead and dine without him. The purpose of so doing is to educate him, should he have any grip on what is going on, or to raise his awareness should he have decent comprehension. There exists a prophetic report with regard to accepting invitations and not keeping the host waiting. The prophet said: If you are invited to a meal, you should accept the invitation. If you are not fasting, you should eat, and even if you are fasting, you should join in. [4] If one who is fasting is commanded to accept such an invitation, then how can one who is not fasting turn it down? How about the one who accepts an invitation but then keeps people waiting? This happened to Jahzah al-Barmaki with a young man. He wrote to him saying: You kept the messenger waiting in distress and asked him to wait longer. You grieved your friends who were ready to eat. You stood them up and starved them to death. [5] It is said that there are three things that are nerve-racking: a lamp that does not give light, a slow messenger, and waiting at a table for a guest running late.

[4] This translation is based on how the word is vocalized in the edited text (fa-l-yasil) as well as the context of the following paragraph. In other renditions of this hadith, the word is vocalized as fa-l-yusalli, "he should pray". It is interpreted as an advice to the invitee to pray for the host, should the former be invited to a meal while fasting.

[5] Literally, you burned their insides because of hunger with an ever-increasing fire.

Continued on page 97

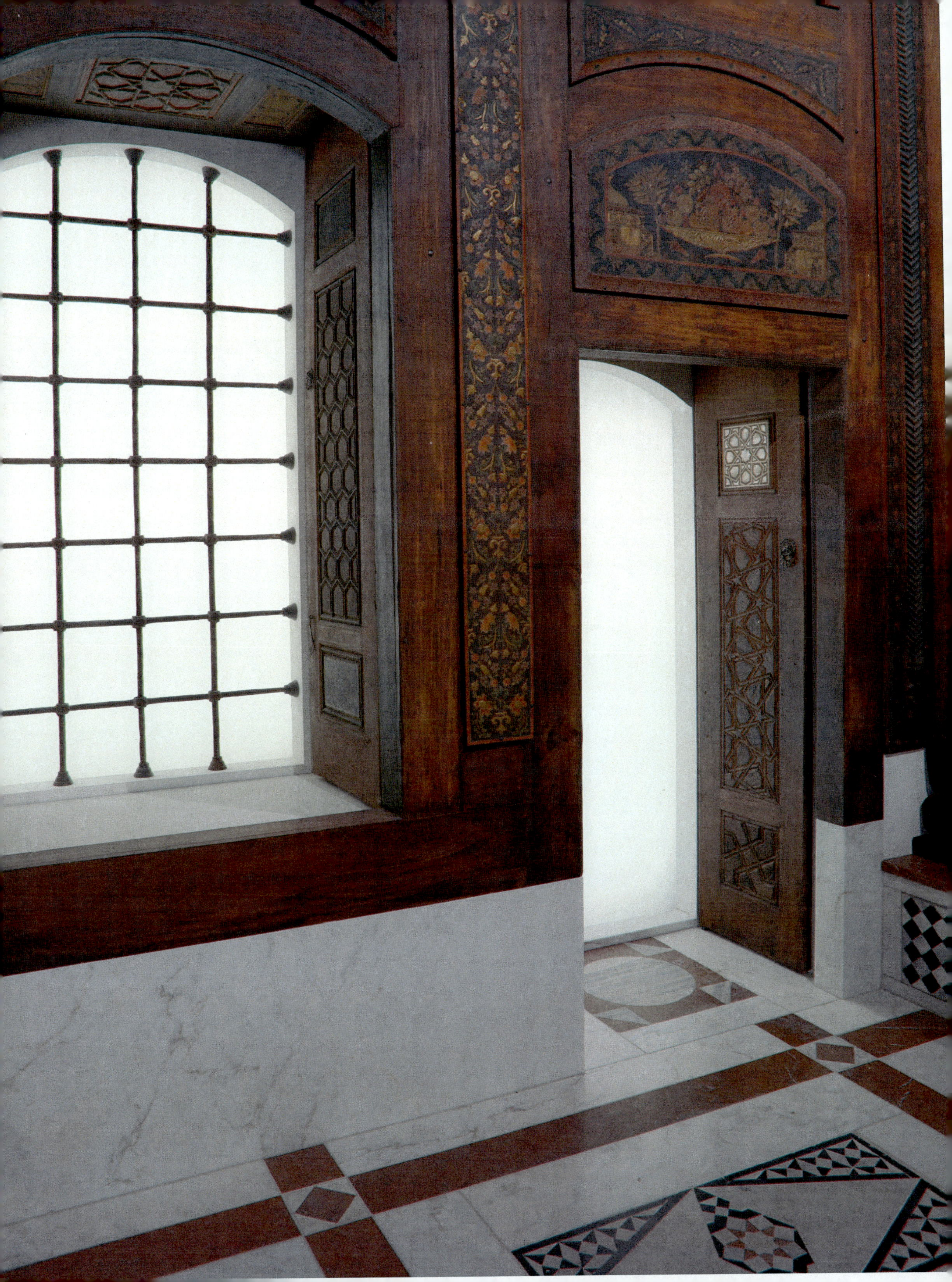

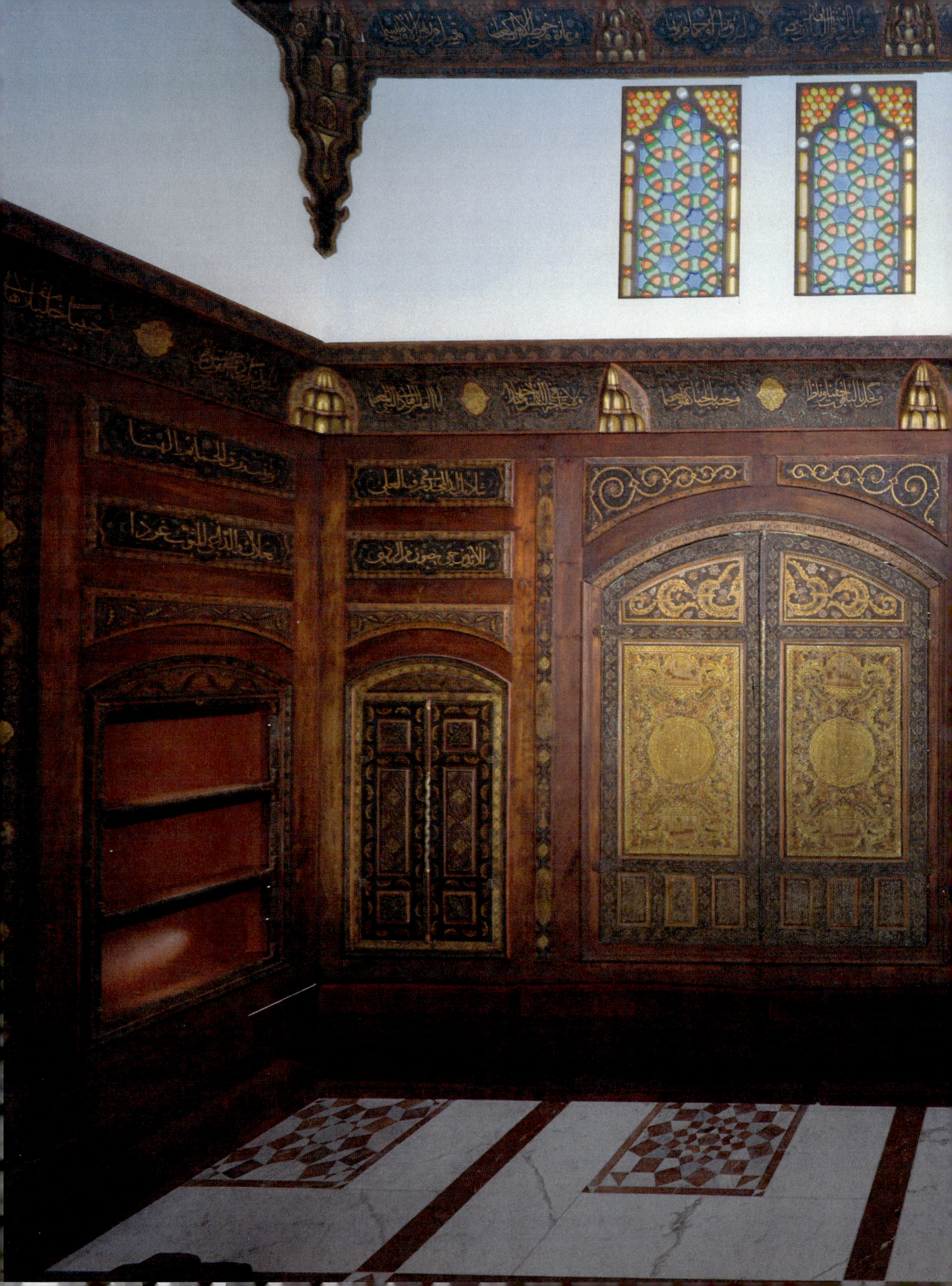

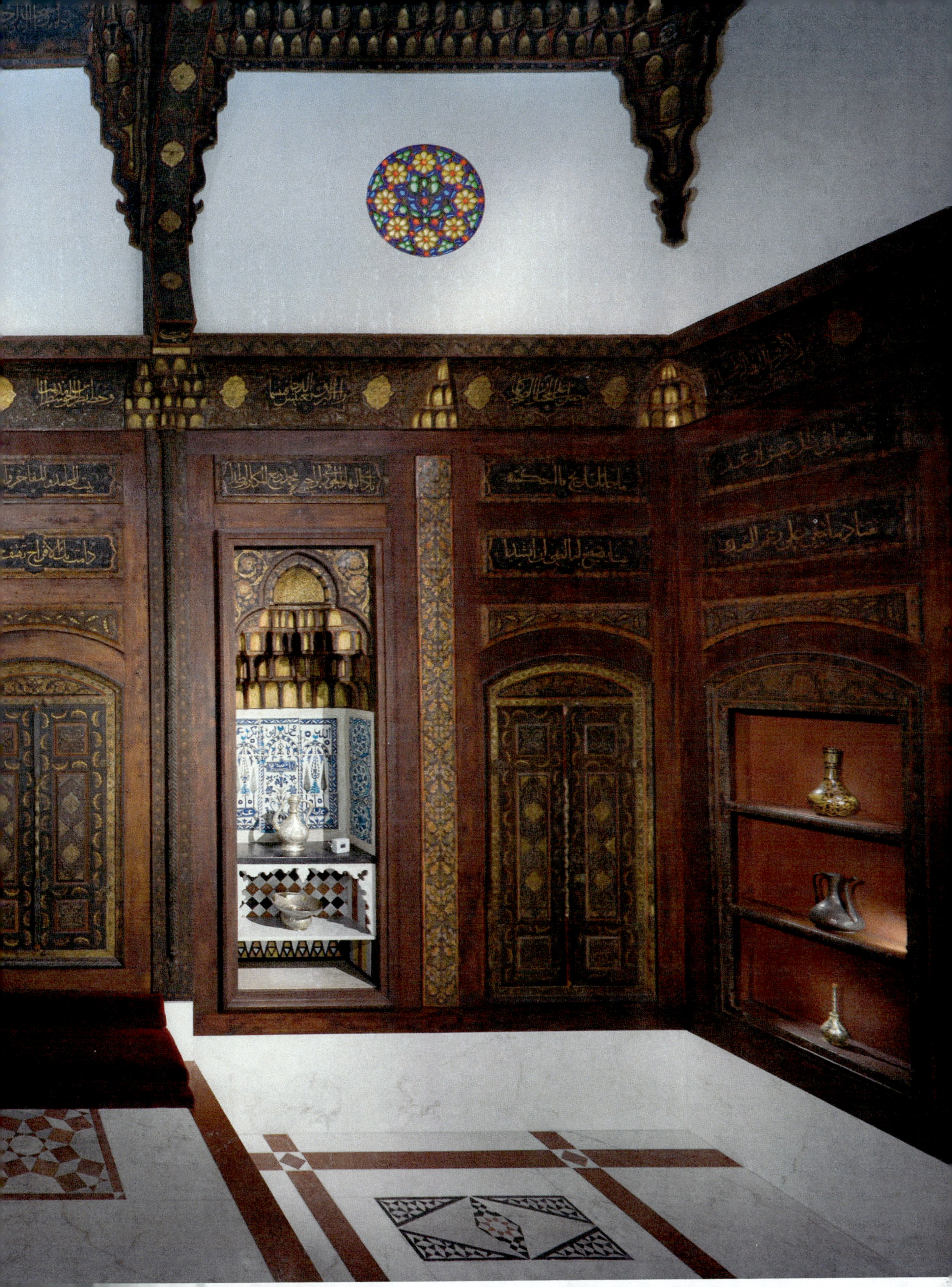

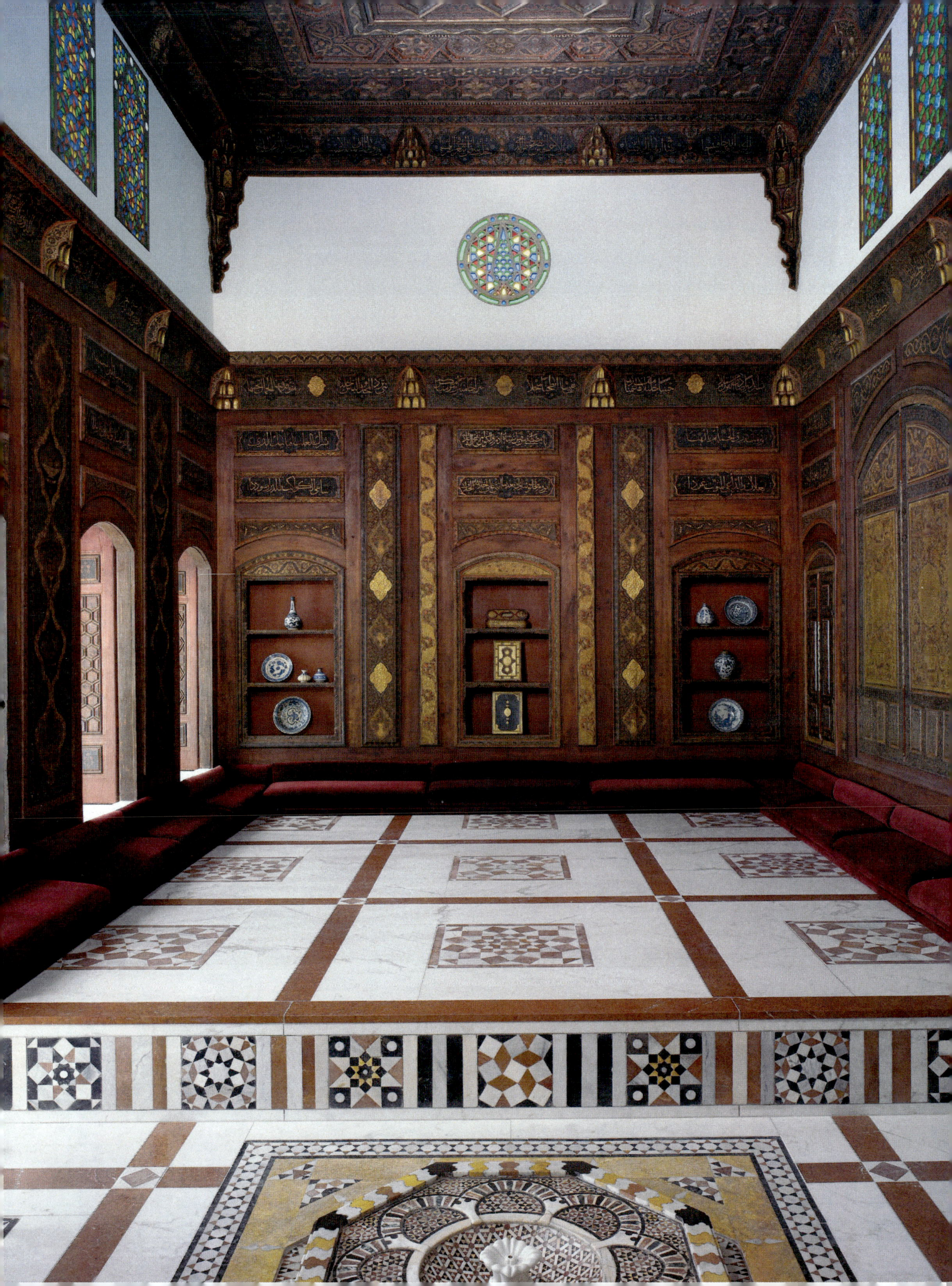

The Grunter (al-muba'bi')

The grunter is one who wants to say something while eating, yet without waiting to swallow his food. The grunter speaks while still chewing and thus grunts like a camel. One cannot understand what he is saying, especially if he has a large bite in his mouth.

The Smacker (al-mufarqi')

The smacker is the one who does not close his lips while chewing, and the sound coming out of his mouth can be heard as far as the front door of the house. He might even spew food from his mouth. Proper etiquette means that even the nearest person should not hear the sound of any chewing.

The Finger-Licker (al-latta' or al-lahhas)

A finger-licker is someone who licks his fingers in order to remove the grease from the food. He does this before finishing and goes back to eating. One can do that after eating; there is nothing wrong with it as long as a person does not continue eating. The best thing to do, if need be, is to wipe one's hands with something like the tablecloth.

The Stretcher (al-mumtadd)

The stretcher is one who eats from a platter far away from him, and in order to do so he ends up stretching and snaking his arm.

The Stomach-turner (al-muqazziz)

The stomach-turner is one who speaks of things at the table that would nauseate his fellow diners. Such a person relates the stories of the infirm and those suffering from diarrhea. He speaks of ulcers, pus, vomit, feces, mucus, and so on. A stomach-turner is also one who constantly blows his nose, burps, and rubs his eyes at the table.

The Camel-neck (al-jamali)

The camel-neck is one who stretches out his neck in order not to drop any broth on his clothes. He cranes his head like a camel, but then he drips from his mouth onto the table and the tablecloth.

The Terminator (al-mukharrib)

The terminator is one who eats everything on a platter, leaving behind nothing but bones. He eats up whatever meat and tasty food he finds without paying any heed to the others, as if he were the sole person at the table.

المُبَعْبِع

اللَّحَّاس

المُقَزِّز

المُخَرِّب

The Setter (*al-musaffif*)

The setter is one who gets to work at setting the table. He puts out the plates and the dishes, thinking this is a service to the guests. This is not the case, as he does so in order to find out what kinds of food there are and to place the tasty ones by his spot at the table.

The Meddlesome (*al-fuduli*)

The meddlesome fellow is one who cannot control himself when he sees a roasted lamb, such that he gets his hands on it and rips it into pieces thinking that he is actually doing something nice by helping the guests. In reality, this bothers the host, for perhaps the host wanted to keep half the lamb intact for whoever wanted it. This is overall a grave shortcoming. It may be that whoever does this intends to gather the best of the meat in front of him. The meddlesome fellow is also the one who goes ahead with breaking the bread and placing it on the table. Similarly, the intention of doing this might be that he wants to gather the best piece of bread in front of himself. He also adds spices and salt to a dish, thus ruining it for his fellow diners by making it too salty. Also, his fellow diners may not like salt at all. He grabs the sauce or vinegar and sprinkles it over *harisah* or similar dishes, oblivious to the fact that there might be guests who dislike this, because they are not used to it. The proper etiquette is not to get involved in what is being served. The setter [see above] is also called meddlesome.

The Glutton (*al-nahim*)

The glutton is the one who constantly stuffs his face. The other guests might take their time coming to the table, but the glutton remains, gorging himself on food. He might chew voraciously, eating twice the amount!

The Racer (*al-musabiq*)

The racer is a type of glutton. He holds a piece of food in his hand before even chewing what he has in his mouth. You would not see his mouth free of chewing and his hand empty. His gaze is always on another morsel.

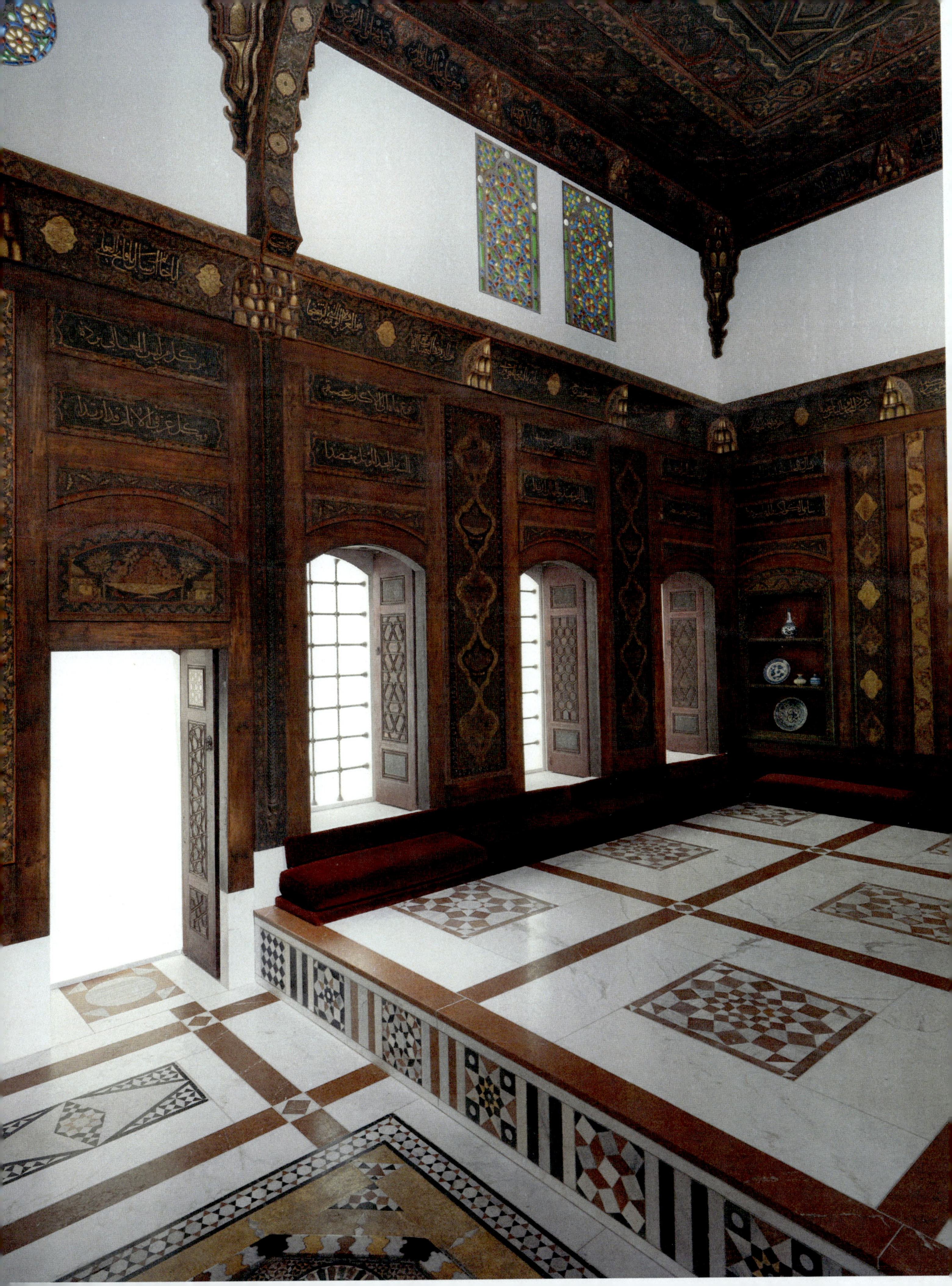

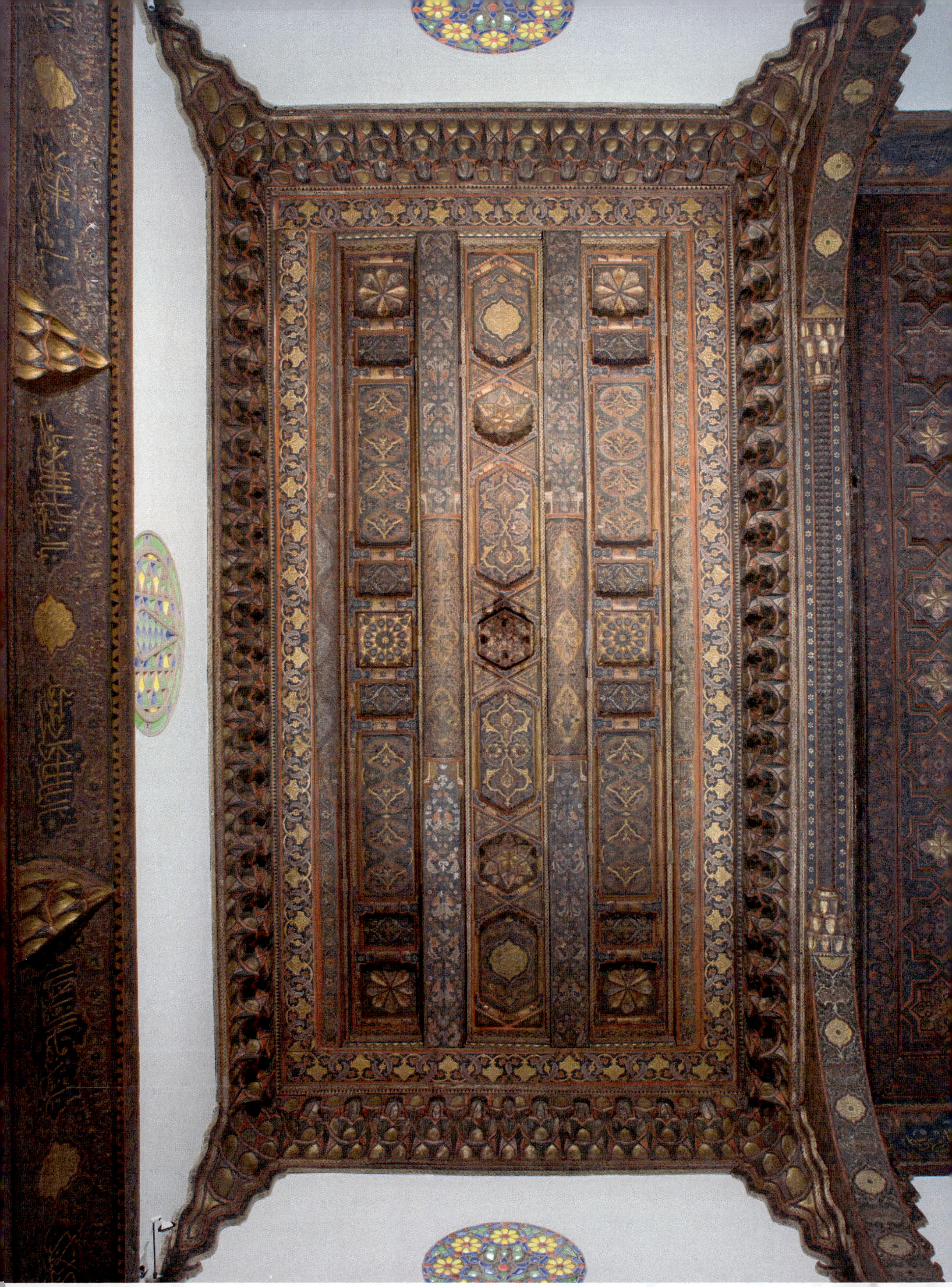

The Heedless (hatib layl)

The heedless fellow is one who does not care what he is eating. He might eat a fly fallen in a dish without noticing, even if other guests point it out. When he eats fish, he does not care to debone it. Most of the time, you find him with a bone stuck in his throat, about to suffer from something unpleasant. Likewise, chicken bones and bones of other birds such as pigeons and smaller birds might get stuck in his throat. In such circumstances, he stops enjoying food and drink and suffers from pain. This happened to the noble sheikh Yusuf b. Ya'qub, who was on the verge of death for twenty days, until he got rid of the bone in his throat.

The Praiser (al-hamid)

الحامِد

The praiser is the one who praises the Almighty out loud in the middle of eating. When this is done, especially by the host, it might be interpreted as a warning to the guests that they should stop eating. **6** Jahzah reported the following experience: A friend was eating with me at my place, and he heard me praising God the Almighty in the middle of our meal. I did so because of one of His innumerable favors, which I'd thought of at that point. My friend stood up and said: By God, I will never join you again. What is the meaning of praising God at this point? It is as if you wanted to inform us that we have eaten enough. My friend then turned to the inkwell and wrote the following poem:

> Praising God is proper at any time,
> But not at the start of a meal.
> For you embarrass your guests
> and suggest they hurry up and finish.
> You annoy them while they haven't eaten their fill.
> This is not what the generous do.

6 *In the Islamic tradition one praises God after eating and/or drinking something. A prayer of praise marks the end of eating.*

وحمدُ الله يَحسُنُ كلَّ وقتٍ ولكن ليس في أول الطعام
لأنك تُحشِمُ الأضيافَ منــه وتأمرهم بإســراع القيام
وتؤذيهمْ وما شَبِعوا بشبعٍ وذلك ليس من خُلُقِ الكرام

The Spewer (al-naththar)

النَّثّار

The spewer is one who laughs out loud with food in his mouth to the extent that his fellow diners can see the chewed food in his mouth, and pieces of it fly out.

The Bovine (al-baqqar)

A bovine fellow is one who sporadically sticks out his tongue like a cow to lick his lips.

The Divider (al-mufarriq)

The divider is one who pushes aside the meat and kababs in a dish to hide them from his fellow guests. He then spoons them out swiftly and stealthily for himself. Such a person is also called a pilferer (*mukhtalis*).

The Disgorger (*al-muʿazzil*)

A disgorger is one who, despite being full, when a new dish is served, vomits in order to eat from it.

The Grumbler (*al-mutashakki*)

The grumbler is a host who complains about drought and the cost of living and apologizes to his guest on account of his poverty. This is worst when done while eating or before food. Abu al-ʿAynaʾ related the following anecdote: I hosted an Arab guest during a drought, and I apologized to him and spoke extensively about the cost of living. He raised his hand and said: It is not fitting for a gentleman to speak about the cost of living in front of his guest while food is being served. I apologized to him and adjured him by God to start eating, but he refused and left the next morning.

The Fidgeter (*al-mutakhallil*)

A fidgeter is one who plays with his nails, hair, beard, and so on.

All praise is due to God, Lord of all the worlds.

NEW BOOKS from
THE LIBRARY OF ARABIC LITERATURE

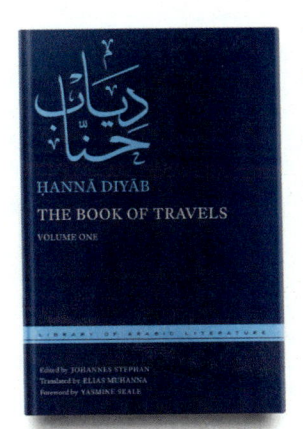

The adventures of the man who created Aladdin

The Book of Travels
by Ḥannā Diyāb
Edited by Johannes Stephan
Translated by Elias Muhanna
Foreword by Yasmine Seale
Afterword by
Paulo Lemos Horta

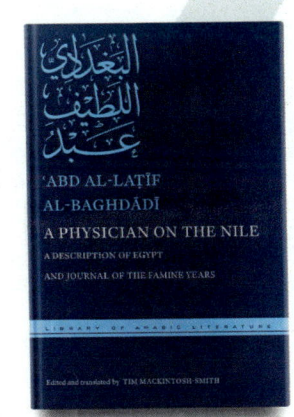

Flora, fauna, and famine in thirteenth-century Egypt

A Physician on the Nile
A Description of Egypt and Journal of the Famine Years
by ʿAbd al-Laṭīf al-Baghdādī
Edited and translated by
Tim Mackintosh-Smith

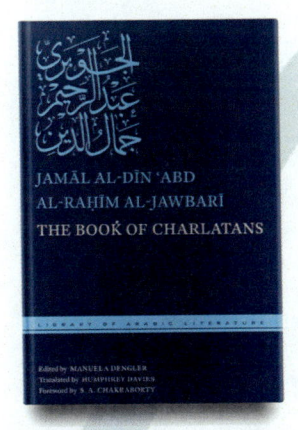

"A mesmerising account of... quacks and tricksters."
—*The Spectator*

The Book of Charlatans
by Jamāl al-Dīn
ʿAbd al-Raḥīm al-Jawbarī
Edited by Manuela Dengler
Translated by
Humphrey Davies
Foreword by
S. A. Chakraborty

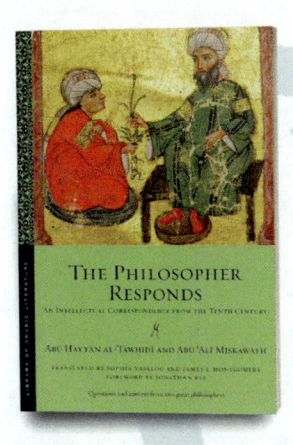

"A fascinating read, particularly for the aspiring scholar of classical Arabic texts."
—*Al Jadid*

The Philosopher Responds
An Intellectual Correspondence from the Tenth Century
by Abū Ḥayyān al-Tawḥīdī and Abū ʿAlī Miskawayh
Translated by Sophia Vasalou and James E. Montgomery
Foreword by Jonathan Rée

Available online or at your local bookstore
WWW.LIBRARYOFARABICLITERATURE.ORG
WWW.NYUPRESS.ORG
WWW.COMBINEDACADEMIC.CO.UK (UK/EUROPE)

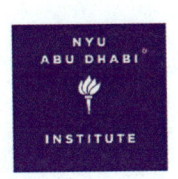

Under grape leaves
Al-Mintar (also Al-Qasr or farm palace) is a type of building that is common in Palestine, intended for farmers to monitor agricultural lands (usually vines and olive fields) during the harvest period. It usually consists of two floors, a ground floor with thick walls made of stone for storing crops, and an upper floor used as a watchtower.
1898
© Library of Congress

Essay

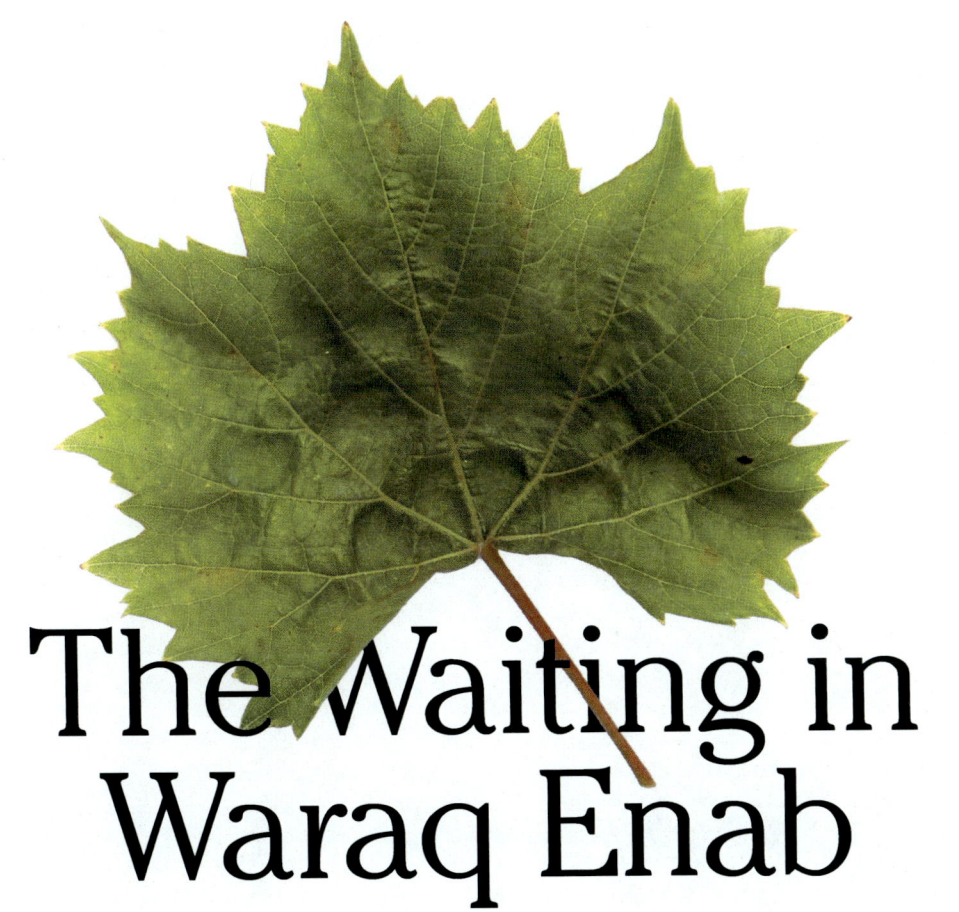

The Waiting in Waraq Enab

By **Yasmine Shamma**

On a gray day, in the middle of the third lockdown, in the middle
of a middling year, in the middle of
another country, I stare at a jar of grape leaves in brine and think,
"The time has come: I will stuff them."

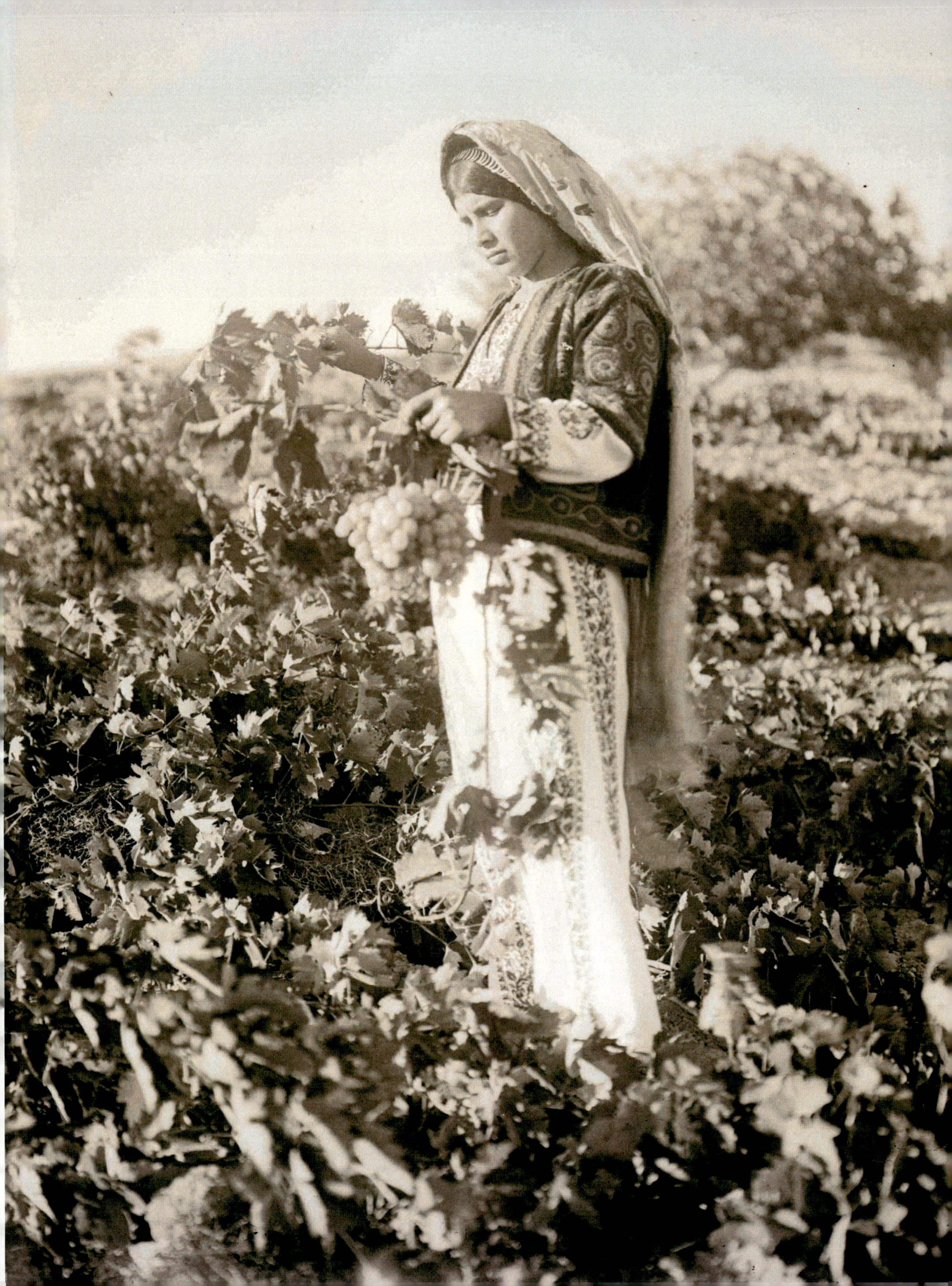

Waraq enab (ورق عِنَب) is the name for the slow-cooked dish of stuffed grape leaves I contemplate making. The "q" of classical Arabic is, colloquially, softly dropped, and the "e" at the start of the word for grape is debatably an "i" or an "ei" as famous Middle Eastern cookbook writer Claudia Roden writes, so that you are saying "wara' eineb." Waraq enab literally means "grape leaves," but the word "waraq" is also Arabic for paper. So in my first-generation Arabic-speaking mind, waraq enab becomes "grape paper." To me, it means a thing you might write a story, or poem, or directions for how to get home on, or the recipe for a much-missed meal.

Waraq enab is my lose-all-sense-of-manners-going-for-seconds-and-thirds-and-fourths meal. Yet in contrast, it is a meal that I shake my head in disappointment at when seeing it listed on a menu, because I know that I will mourn my grandmother's version as I eat any restaurant's rendition. "This is not my grandmother's way," I want to say whenever I'm offered a fat, overstuffed, cold, oily, loosely rolled waraq enab in a supposedly "authentic" restaurant. What's worse is that these phony rolls do not, as the theory has it, satiate nostalgia. Rather, they perpetuate it.

"Behind the assiduous documentation and defense of the authentic lies an unarticulated anxiety of losing the subject," Regina Bendix writes, in *In Search of Authenticity*, and an essay by Anita Mannur on "Culinary Nostalgia" complicates nationalism in cooking. Mannur explains that in food-concerned memories of an immigrant's home and/or past, "[the] desire to simultaneously embrace what is left of a past from which one is spatially and temporally displaced, and the recognition that nostalgia can overwhelm memories of the past, allow … the colors of history to seep out of the mind's eye." That is, not-my-grandmother's-waraq-enab makes me miss her more, because in eating something that feigns to remind me of her, I am reminded not of her but of the gap between the signifier and the thing. Grape leaves do not bring me closer to her. They painfully articulate how far away I am from her, and even further still from the notions of "home" that women like her signify.

So, instead, I practice waiting. I order something else, I make something else; I stuff the grape leaves, not with their traditional meat stuffing, but with a longing that threatens the labor latent in even the consideration of writing this piece and making that dish.

Stewing

The delicate stuffing of what we call waraq enab is a process of care; a tedious, delicate kind of conjuring, which often takes slow place rebelliously in fast-paced spaces of displacement. Eating it feels like an act not of consumption, but of preservation. But when meals preserve you—your sense of self and heritage—in their making, what does it mean for them to feel unmakeable? What happens when the "out of place" cook, to borrow a phrase from Edward Said, dares to stew this displacement on a stovetop far away?

I miss the sense of home enveloped within meals like waraq enab. But the children are hungry, and a jar of peanut butter looms with an ease and convenience that confronts me with bigger questions: Will making the fast meal rather than the slow one perpetuate generational displacement? I try to remember whether my children have ever even *had* waraq enab, and recognize that my doing so perpetuates my own procrastination more than their displacement.

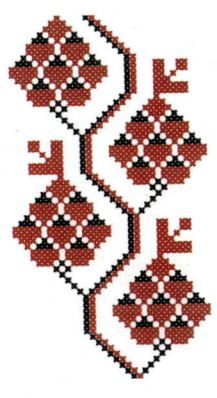

Grape leaves motif
in Palestinian embroidery

Grape leaves don't traditionally represent delay, but they do carry with them the weight of a ceremony that so many of us, whether home or away, know as a fact of daily life: waiting. Waiting can be wonderful; it can be pregnant with excitement; it can propel desire. But it can also, and especially for those in the diaspora, be existentially exhausting. With waraq enab, there is the delicate rolling and careful arranging, which carries with it that excitement, and then there is the stewing, which seems to be unbracketed. I am exhausted from making waraq enab before I even begin, because it is not just technically time-consuming, but emotionally so—far more loaded than a peanut-butter sandwich.

My sister's name flashes on my phone, and I answer with an enthusiasm for the distraction conveniently being brought *to* me. I tell her what I'm thinking of doing. She laughs with the kind of cackle only sisters accept as communal instead of insulting. "You mean you're thinking of *not* making waraq enab?" She's both right, and, despite the affectionate betrayal implied in her laugh, empathetic—she is not shocked that I've been thinking about the meal in general. Rather, she confesses that from her own locked-down position *within* Lebanon, she's been having dreams about it. In one, she discovered that everyone had been serving the dish from frozen all along. At this point, I laugh, not at her dream, but at her subconscious trying to find the trick to shorten the time between desire and consumption.

Hebron Grape
Lithography
Troncy Viala Vermorel
1910

Cookbook writer Joudie Kalla warns: "making it is a labour of love," and anyone who has watched their teta or grandmother spend the morning rolling knows this. As I belabor the time required for this meal, it is not lost on me that this is a form of delaying the moment, as I've been doing since I purchased the jar of grape leaves over a year ago. I call my mother "for research purposes." She responds: "You know you don't traditionally make waraq enab in a pressure-cooker. It takes time. Many an expert has failed at this dish: Too tight, too loose, not enough rice, too much rice. It takes time." My mother repeats the word "time" as a warning. As my children look on, the elder of the two nods along to the FaceTime, as if to remind me—as if his gorgeous existence didn't remind me every guilt-ridden moment—that I never have time. The younger responds with the less delicate urgency of a second-born, "but I'm hungry now." I look at them and we all share the knowledge that, according to history, I will make something else, and in so doing I will continue my process of delay with this jar of grape leaves.

Place

Waraq enab does not easily accept any national assignment. In a region divided by the lines of nation-states, the dish quietly looms extra-territorial. The roots of stuffed grape leaves lay muddled in that rich and ancient landscape we gesture toward when we say "Mediterranean." Greeks have a stuffed-grape-leaf dish called "dolmans," Turks have a similar one called "dolma" or "sarma." Lebanese refer to their stuffed, warm grape leaves as "waraq enab"; Palestinians as "waraq dawali"; Jordanians sometimes call their iteration of the dish, and any other stuffed vegetable, simply "mahshi", meaning "stuffed." Though the names and ingredients vary, they all come out looking more or less like fat cigarettes or fingers, with rice, diced tomatoes, and often meat inside, carefully rolled, then layered, then stewed. Though one is prone to wanting the dish as one knows it, it's possible to take solace in the ways the dish resists nationalization.

Ampélographie.

Hébron

I pick up the jar I purchased at the local "Istanbul Market" and hope a glimmer of white is a preventative mold in the leaves. I drift with the jar, not to the meal, but to their source—"Istanbul Market," our local ethnic grocery store. When one finds a place offering ingredients from their original home, they feel at home. I remember finally feeling at "home" in Florida when a friend told me about "Food Town." Shamelessly, "Food Town" lumped all the ethnic "others" of south Florida into an American-style grocery store, with each ethnic food region allotted an aisle. The Middle East was between Indian and Jamaican. No one seemed to mind this lumping. Instead, you'd find yourself giving or receiving a knowing nod as you sifted through the variety of spices that delineated your home from another's. "Food Town" made us all one big lost person, enveloped by the strange comfort of turmeric in the air. There is an unspoken code when entering these foreign delis and shops: an accessibility, not to that departed "home," but to a sense of communal appreciation for the space between you and it, filled in the meantime with overpriced baklava, bottles of orange-blossom water, bags of basmati, and jars of grape leaves.

My daydream of transnational grocery shopping is interrupted by a knock at the door. It is Nikos, the window-cleaner. Because of his name, I knew he'd be Greek and that, as an immigrant, his dropping a flier at my door the day before demonstrated a work ethic, will, and silent suffering of daily, perpetual microaggressions for being "other" in a country that had just voted to rule "others" out. With one hand holding the door open, and the other holding this murky glass jar of grape leaves, we talked about the glass that needed cleaning. Nikos asks me where I'm from. Innocuous, spiraling question that it is, I've learned that the answer is dependent upon the audience: just as I know that Nikos is a Greek name, he knows that mine comes from nearby. I choose the easier of the two parental homelands to associate with: "Lebanon," I say, tripling the syllables for foreigners and estranging myself from the true name of the country, *Lubnan*. He smiles and says, "Ah, the food!" and I smile as if I hadn't predicted his response. "So similar to ours!" he continues, and we spend 15 more minutes of delay in the doorway, talking about how to find the best dolma/waraq enab in town. "Good?" he asks when I query his recent experience at the Lebanese taverna, "Get out of here, it's amazing!"

"I wish I could get out of here," I say, and we both laugh underneath our masks, knowing that we can't. "Home," I find myself daring to define, "makes you hungry."

Nikos gets to work on the windows, and I sit myself down with the grape leaves of this essay. Food historians, cultural anthropologists, postcolonial literary scholars, and philosophers all treat national foods as emblems of a parseable piece of that nation, carried in body and mind, by the immigrant subject. In "Culinary Nostalgia," Mannur writes of the ways in which the creators and eaters of national foods outside their nations engage in "the desire to simultaneously embrace what is left of a past from which one is spatially and temporally displaced and the recognition that nostalgia can overwhelm memories of the past, allowing the colours of history to seep out of the mind's eye."

My mother FaceTimes me from Amman, which is her space of displacement (and that of so many other Palestinians). She is calling to see how the meal is coming along. I tell her (because there's nothing to show) my evolving theory about waraq enab's anational transcendence. "عم بتلفي وتدوري" she warns, meaning that I am getting lost and losing myself, although it more precisely translates to "you are rolling and spinning [in circles]." I willfully roll words together, rather than leaves, and reiterate that maybe waraq enab comes from our motherlands, and that, like maternity, such a concept may serve as its own kind of place.

Waraq enab is, to me, my maternal grandmother's dish. Though both made it, Teta Giselle made it best—made it better than anyone, and as I write this, I fear I have caused my paternal Teta Inayat to roll over in her grave. But I can still see Teta Giselle's red طنجرة "tanjera" cooking pot and feel again the awe of watching her, seemingly all day, working in a kitchen, displaced in Amman, that had a density unknowable beyond it. It was three by six, yet could feed what felt like a nation, or more precisely five children, 12 grandchildren, exponentially still multiplying great-grandchildren, and any passing neighbor.

Spells

When I seek a recipe—nay *the* recipe of the hybrid Teta Giselle—I find others, written by other hybrid, displaced people. Mandy Shunnarah's "Grape Leaves" makes this point. Shunnarah writes not only of missing her grandmother and her grape leaves after her death, but of her grandfather missing her too—epitomized in a nostalgia for waraq enab:

> … When he tasted the grape leaves, with their soft rice, tomato and dried mint seasoned lamb, and the slight lemony flavor of the leaves, he said nothing—only closed his eyes, thinking of his dead wife, a rare smile edging itself into the corners of his mouth.

As Shunnarah continues, she imagines trying to make the recipe, but laments that though she witnessed its making over the years, she never attained it herself:

> Given my young age at the time of Teta's death, cooking grape leaves was not yet a part of my education on How to Be a (Half) Palestinian Woman… cooking grape leaves was, as yet, absent from my curriculum.

This ache is a common refrain in essays that dare to disentangle a recipe from its memory. Memory mingles with longing in my own experience of trying to capture the recipes of my grandmothers, and I become convinced that the reason I'm not making it is because I don't have the "authentic" recipe (for waraq enab; for comfort) at hand. When I ask my mother for her own mother's exact recipe, she stuffs the line with delay: "She never wrote it down. These are things you don't write. They are givens." I know in my heart and fingers how to make waraq enab. But I also wish I had it written down, to ground me in the experience of re-creating those "givens."

Although it may be a stretch to suggest that waraq enab is intoxicating, it may be less of one to call the dish magical. So much so that it can transcend and act as a magical portal: Shunnarah's speaker explains how it felt to have found her grandmother's recipe seemingly reproduced at a random restaurant, "[their] grape leaves could have been made with her exact recipe, right down to the yogurt. It is not an exaggeration to say I all but wept into my plate. Comfort and memory and grief commingled in the dish." Instead of passing on written recipes, we (immigrant novice cooks) pass on spells: the dissolution of written recipes into that hazy realm called memory and remembering. In this, there is a magic and, as with all magic, a loss.

The brand of this loss evades, further propelling its sense of dissolution. Is it a loss of home? In Naomi Shihab-Nye's "My Father and the Figtree," the Arab-American poet describes her displaced father who never felt quite at home because, "years passed, we lived in many houses, none had figtrees." The father tries to explain what the fig means to him:

> "I'm talking about picking the largest fattest sweetest fig
> in the world and putting it in my mouth."
> (Here he'd stop and close his eyes.)

Have you been brought to weep by food? Have you been brought to "stop and close" your eyes by a food or concoction of ingredients commingling time, place, self, and sense? The last time you had a macaron in Paris, that bagel on a bench in New York, that brioche stuffed with halloum packed away by your grandmother to be consumed on a layover in Amsterdam, the manousheh of Beirut, the frying of fish on Falmouth, the waraq enab of your displaced and now diffused Palestinian grandmother in Amman? These meals cannot but coalesce with the situations that bore them, so how can they ever be recreated? And if the simple answer is that, like a river that cannot be stepped in twice, you cannot ever have the same waraq enab you had at that small melamine table in your grandmother's kitchen in 1993, then what can we expect of the plagued process of desire in opening a recipe book, or this jar beside me, but for the tears to be realer than those brought on by onions?

In *The Meaning of Food,* the editors focus on the abstracting possibilities of "foodways," explaining that "everything about eating including what we consume, how we acquire it, who prepares it and who's at the table—is a form of communication rich with meaning. Our attitudes, practices and rituals around food are a window into our most basic beliefs about the world and ourselves." In *Cooking a Home*, Pilar Puig Cortada explains that she took to composing a narrative book of recipes by Syrian refugees as a way of continuing comforting conversations with the refugees she met in the camps. I too have had the privilege of spending time speaking to Syrian refugees in the camps of Jordan and have slipped, like Cortada, into "the comfort and joy" of talking to them about the food they would often have been in the middle of preparing when I'd interrupted them. The tendency had been, it seemed, to cook things that took time, because there was so much of it.

On my last visit to the camps, I had a conversation with a woman and her sister, Nora and Lina, [1] who sat on the floor carefully stuffing eggplants while I interviewed them. When I asked them why they chose to make a meal of pickled eggplants—a literal act of preservation—Nora explained with a laugh that they had time on their hands, and that the meal they were making, makdous, reminded them of home. Their "most basic belief" about their identities in food was that you could take the cook out of her home, but home remained as long as she was cooking. The eggplants and waraq enab would continue throughout Nora's and Lina's lives to be stuffed and rolled, regardless of their physical locations. [2]

During the five years I spent interviewing refugees of the Syrian crisis, I asked them what "home" means. I remain confounded by two counterpoints: 1. that the refugees I've spoken to rarely mention the names of the countries they left and lost; and 2. that Arabic lacks a specific word for "home." When I've offered "beit" (house) in conversation, it is

[1] *These are pseudonyms to preserve privacy and anonymity.*

[2] *makinghomeaway.com*

often corrected and expanded in responses, with refugees tending to use instead the word *balad*, which, like so many Arabic words, means many things in a mere three letters (ب/ل/د). Among them: country, place, city, village, community. They also tend, more often than not, to inflect it with the plural possessive "balad*na*": our place, our community. These interviews remind me, among other things, of the perpetuity of displacement; of how the sounds in *baladna* get elongated over generations. Of how sad a word can be in its vowels.

The grape leaves begin to weep a little when I set them beside baladna. In the context of a lost land, both the "enab" and the "waraq" feel imbued with homesickness. Though they wish to carry within them the possibility of a cure, they perpetuate the unending insatiability of displacement. But they also unite. Not unlike the better-known olive, mention of a plate of good grape leaves brings together the knowing, aching half-smiles of migrants and immigrants from an entire vineyard-speckled segment of the earth.

Time

Grape leaves, preserved in brine, lay on a cutting board or plate, to be stuffed with a pre-concocted mix, rolled not-too-tight and not-too-loose, then stewed with the brine of lemon and tomatoes, tasted between hours. Like the "labor" implied in so many of the recipes that mention how long it takes to make this dish, these acts of care know their end is worth their wait. Like the writing of a recipe or a poem, they outlive their initial consumption. And though they suggest they'll satiate decade-long cravings, recipes for missed dishes often exchange the cravings of the tongue for the cravings of the heart—engaging their consumer in a perpetuation of longing as a side to the displacement which bore the craving to begin with.

In an essay on culinary practice and diasporic identity, "Food to Remember: Culinary Practice and Diasporic Identity," Razia Parveen argues that recipes constitute oral histories—and that they bind over time. In reading a description of how to make the Pakistani dish pinnia, she explains:

> A clear message is transmitted: that nothing of value is achieved without effort. The shaping of this recipe is not an individual act (or decision), but the product of shared effort between teacher and student and many women's voices over generations. Maria is not just remembering her mother, but she is also remembering for her mother. Successive maternal voices, evoked from another time and place, bind the community together and are sought after in diaspora.

Maternal, binding, time, place, successive, generations, shared—I associate all these words with waraq enab and the recipes I seek and cannot find. For though my grandmother kept a recipe book, waraq enab is missing. As my mother, her daughter, reminds me, "it is a given."

My mother didn't make us waraq enab growing up. Though she cooked and still cooks, endlessly and deliciously, an almost purely Middle Eastern repertoire, I cannot recall a single time she made waraq enab. Yet I still call her for the recipe. And when she implies that it takes more time than I have to give, she is referring not just to my seeming impatience, or to my delinquency as a conventional housewife, but to other forms of prolonged, protracted, painful time. Even a recent children's book, Kathy Camper's *Ten Ways to Hear the Snow*, makes a point of exploring the maternal bond of cooking grape leaves with a grandmother as an elastic, time-honored and time-expanding experience, as it imagines the ways the world stays still while such long processes of cooking are engaged. In the book, a child walks through a snowy neighborhood to their grandmother's house and encounters a world of experiences—all while, in the background, the grape leaves are ostensibly cooking. The book suggests that the duration of preparing waraq enab is both comforting and generative in its unending-ness.

This play of time—the long and the short of it, and its framing within political contexts of seemingly never-ending strife and waiting for strife to end—is made manifest in the final scene of one of the many delicately rendered visions of Palestinian life by film-maker Elia Suleiman. In *Divine Intervention*, a mother and son sit staring at a pressure cooker, in silence. Like many of the film's frames, this silent rendering allows just enough time for the viewer to wonder if the pressure cooker is Palestine, before the moment is punctuated by a confirming direction from the mother: خلاص ماما بيكفيها —"Stop it mama, that's enough for it." It's almost redundant, because "bi kafeeha" has in it the sense of finitude, and "khalas" belabors the point, while "mama" has its own doubleness. When a parent speaks this colloquialism to their child affectionately, with a tinge of intended persuasion, they will often use this reflexive mode of speech— calling the child by the name the child would call them: "mama," in this instance. As a child this befuddled me, and, raised abroad, my own parents never did it. When we'd return to Jordan and Lebanon for our summers I'd hear children called "mama" and "baba" and I didn't understand it, though somewhere I also did—the call to be a mother, for that moment, permits the child to look back at the mother, to be truly for a moment empathetic with the mother's request, while also linguistically enacting a symbiosis. In Suleiman's *Divine Intervention*, the scene with the mother figure's plea to take the pressure-cooker off the heat is also an invitation to the child-figure, to assume a growing-up, to inherit responsibility; to know when something has gone on too long, and do the mature thing of recognizing its need to end. It—Palestine, the speaker, the child, the film rendering it all—is at risk of burning out. It has had enough of its prolonged pressure cooking.

I think of this scene as I imagine approaching the end of my longed-for recipe, and this musing on that recipe, because waraq enab's final step is to lay the assimilated, stuffed rolls tightly, in layers, holding them together through the tension of their proximity, because if you don't they could unfurl. They lay, packed together, in an old tanjera like my grandmother's, or a pressure cooker if you must. Not unlike Palestinians. Indeed in an interview with France 24 about his most recent film, *It Must be Heaven*, Suleiman explains his turn to the global stage: "I think it was more necessary now to consider the world a 'global Palestine'—there is tension everywhere … and there's states of emergency everywhere, and there's police everywhere." Ironically, Suleiman spoke these words only a month before the world began to lock itself down and truly—though crucially, *momentarily*—began to understand his implications of a "global Palestine." The untapped possibility of our prolonged lockdowns has been to cultivate a culture of care; a possibility of transcendental empathy for those who suffer lockdowns their whole lives, living in literally locked-down countries and geographies. We have had, in our respective and collective moments of despair, the possibility of

www.sonachgefuehl.de

understanding, or even caring to understand, what residents and migrants of perpetually unsafe countries and situations suffer through. Yet we've chosen, somewhat unilaterally, to look away, to turn inwards in self-absorption.

We had the opportunity to care, and I have the opportunity to construct this dish-of-motherland, and do not. I am horrified, as I dally, to find that you can order a waraq enab rolling machine online. Instead of engaging in time-taking acts of care, we are wont to make machines that do what our fingers once knew by heart. Instead of devoting a Saturday morning to sitting with my children at the kitchen table, I contemplate how many days away I am from yelling, "Alexa, make me waraq enab." For we repeatedly refute, undervalue, and set aside not just care, but cultures of care. I am doing this in staring at the jar of grape leaves instead of cooking them: I appreciate their metaphoric weight, even their physical weight, but there is a care that I am falling short of—in not creating this dish for my own children, in not valuing the significance of sitting at a table and teaching them, in turn, how to roll a leaf with love, for unending hours, and tuning out the tick-tock of the clock on the wall with a harmonizing hum as we roll up our longing together.

It is this singular ingredient that seems to consistently evade me: time. Even the recipe books list "time" unofficially as the most essential of ingredients. Kalla warns of needing time thrice on a single page and warns: "Be prepared to sit in the same spot for awhile." Then again, "Waraq Inab should be made in a relaxed atmosphere," this time weaving into the recipe of the dish, a recipe for remembering: "… with the music on in the background, recalling memories of the dish as you have eaten it before." It is not just time that I am short on, but the propensity to "relax" and let myself remember, allowing myself to have soulful music on in the background in surrender. I could make manousheh instead, if I trade the grape leaves for the dried thyme ones of zaatar.

I am almost out of the zaatar I'd hoarded over years of incessant travel, weary with nostalgia for lost lands and time. And though enough time has passed for even zaatar to be sold in my local Waitrose, when I think of purchasing it from a British supermarket chain rather than taking it from my aunt's hand-picked bundle off the table in her kitchen, I engage in the same kind of visceral refusal as that which occurs when I see "waraq enab" offered on a menu abroad. So I go, with a mix of hunger and frustration, wanting these things without having them. There is an Arabic expression for this feeling, and conveniently, it embodies an unrolling. When I first heard it uttered by an aunt in a smoky living room brimming with the scent of Turkish coffee at what must have been the always four o'clock of Beirut—a time when exactly nothing wants to be done—I was mesmerized by the possibilities the phrase permitted: فرطت روحي. Resisting translation, like what it stands for, it means, loosely, "my soul has become undone." Which means, I can't take it anymore—or your soul in your body wants to get out. A necklace can do this—it can *tufrut*—if all the beads explode off of it and fall to the ground. An improperly stuffed grape leaf might, too.

The reason I prefer my Palestinian grandmother's rendition of the dish is, quite simply, because her leaves were rolled tighter. I don't know how she did this, because she was known more for her loose laugh than a sense of suppression. But what she accomplished in her version of the dish is a holding—a pulling together of materials and a keeping together of things, free of strain. As my own mother's voice reminds me, "too loose, and they'll fall apart; too tight and they'll break."

Like the ideal stuffed grape leaves, homesickness makes you both delicate and firm. It was my husband who so thoughtfully yet naively gave me *Palestine on a Plate*, and the thoughtfulness was in knowing what I was craving—not just the food but the idea of a place, and the naivety was in thinking that my not making it was due to lacking a recipe. It was not an invitation to cook—my husband will happily cook any day and his cooking is apolitical, unfettered by the plague that affects my grape leaves. But in choosing this specific cookbook, he was trying to invite me to let myself be Palestinian, or Lebanese, or an Arab abroad, here and now—to be at home in this home we made, away. By now, with twenty or so years of independent living under my belt, I could have cooked waraq enab any day of the week, but every day I choose, instead, not to. Now I am possessed by this urge to cook a thing I believe I cannot. Grape leaves are my memory's gateway drug: an invitation to slip, as Kenneth Koch puts it in "One Train May Hide Another," into a "reverse succession of contemplated entities" and in so doing, perpetuate delay. I skip from the strongest memory in my mind to the most recent one, of watching them be stuffed and rolled: on the floor of a tent, on the plastic-covered dirt floor in Zaatari refugee camp; a communal effort between displaced, rightless people during the passing of a quiet afternoon in the nowhere of limbo.

The refugees I met in the camps in Jordan were engaged not only in the rolling of grape leaves, but in the stuffing of various other humble vegetables—those mini eggplants for pickling, small zucchini for stewing, the delicate rolling of cabbage leaves, their slow tender cooking. They engage in these daily ceremonies that require a watchful waiting, an awareness of what they demand, but a silence and acceptance of the duration of that demand. Though I long to hold the home these dishes embody, why can I not embrace the time they take to make?

Having read the reviews of Kalla's book, I want to take issue not with the seemingly "daring" use of the word Palestine in its title, but rather with its audacity in proclaiming to know and possess that country, which has become more than nation and more than place: "Palestine on a Plate." Whichever side of the wall you are on, saying "Palestine" conjures, like its recipes, intense emotions. When Polish poet Adam Zagajewski writes in his near-perfect description of homesickness, "To Go to Lvov," he does so with a crescendo in the refrain: "to go to…" where the reader knows to insert "home." By the poem's end, you arrive not at Lvov, but at that emblem of diaspora: "why must every city / become Jerusalem, and every man a Jew." Zagajewski asks this question without a question mark, and the statement becomes loaded with punctuation that doesn't yet exist, when one's *actual* heritage happens to stem from the actual, tangible Jerusalem.

Zagaweski's poem is strangely hungry for mention of food, but it does end with this:

> pack, always, each day,
> and go breathless, go to Lvov, after all
> it exists, quiet and pure as
> a peach. It is everywhere.

We are taught in school, by rota, that similes compare two like or unlike things. That home in this poem can condense into a fruit, like Shihab-Nye's "fig," that then evaporates into "everywhere," is the poem's feat. It is also, possibly, that of the displaced person.

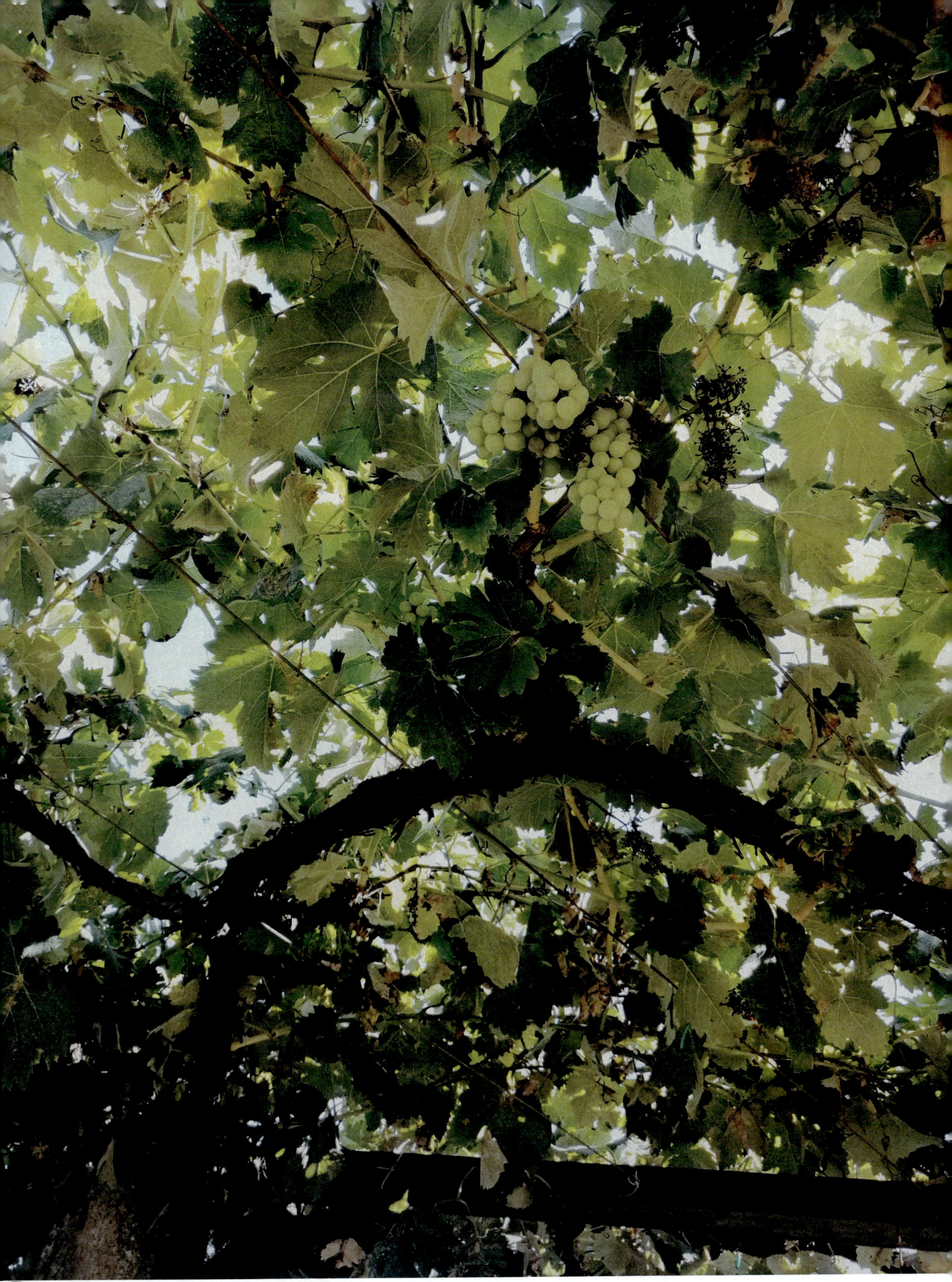

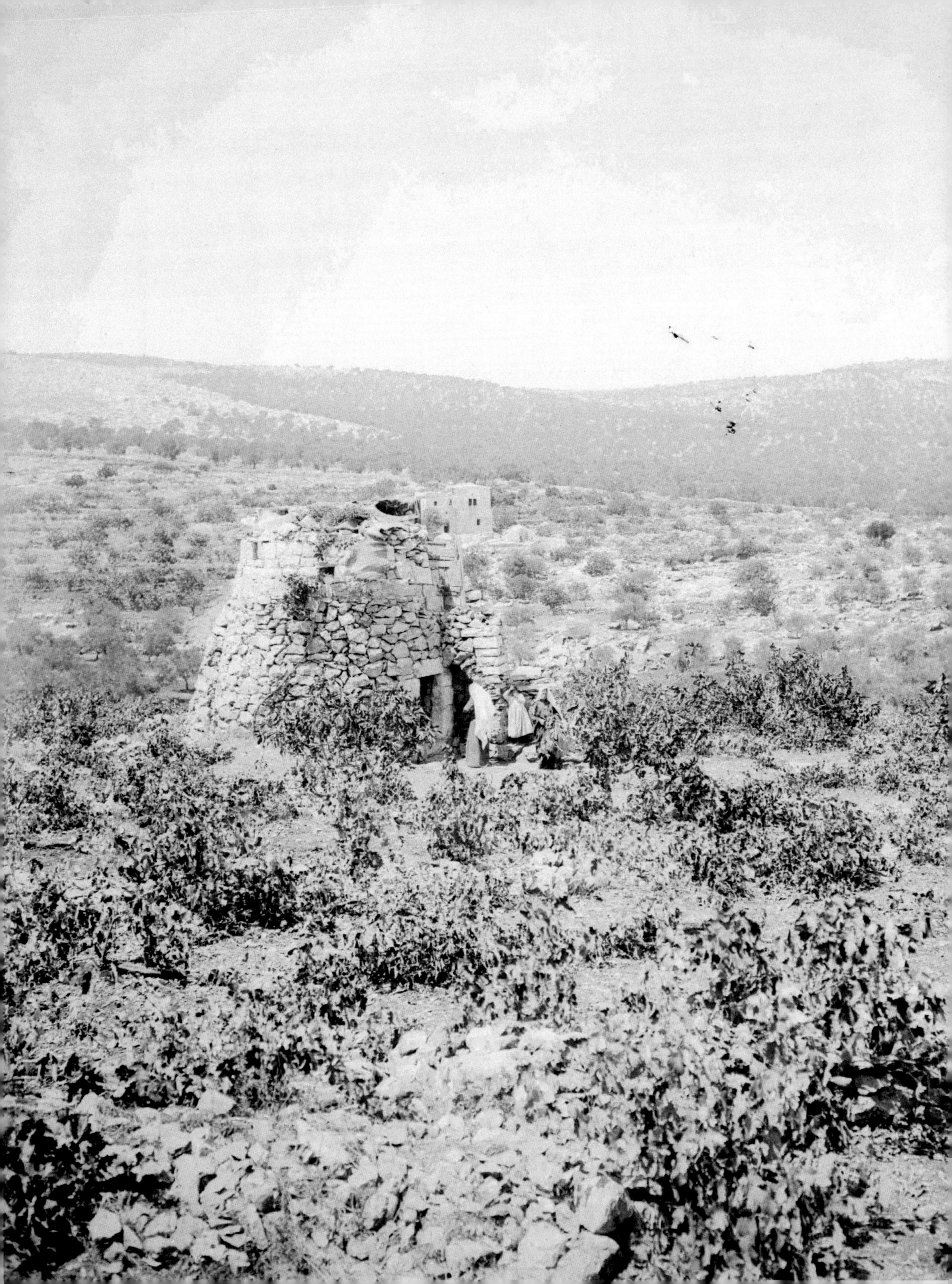

The Persian poet Rumi, who himself emigrated and lived in diaspora, offers another version of this metamorphosis from alienation to universal belonging through none other than our humble grape leaves. In "The Worm's Waking," in Coleman Banks' loose translation, Rumi tells "how a human being can change" through the anecdote of a worm who is "addicted to eating / grape leaves":

> Suddenly he wakes up.
> Call it grace, whatever, something
> wakes him, and he's no longer
> a worm.
>   He's the entire vineyard,
> and the orchard too, the fruit, the trunks,
> a growing wisdom and joy
> that doesn't need
> to devour.

I am addicted to the *idea* of eating grape leaves. I am hungry for them, with a sort of debilitating respect and celebration that stops me from the consumption, while also leaving me musing on the ways in which the hunger might, in all its complexity, be reminiscent of the unending hunger I've come to understand—through refugees, through mothers, through grandmothers—of displacement.

I shake the jar as if to clarify its spell. It gets murkier. I place it on the kitchen table, as a centerpiece that threatens to be finally properly used at some point today. The children's hunger has been satisfied, neither with waraq enab nor with the problematic counterpoint of peanut-butter sandwiches, but instead through a hybrid fix: my own slap-dash rendition of manousheh, made with the last of the zaatar, Spanish olive oil, and store-bought naan bread. It is not the thing itself, but the symbol of a thing, and as such, it holds: the children are eating something that represents something else, and the gesture suffices. Nikos is done cleaning my windows and I wish I had by now cooked *the* dish I crave sharing with him—maybe we'd both then be transported to an elsewhere, like the worm's, and the fig's, and the peach's that is "everywhere." Because Nikos is Mediterranean, it would not be strange to either of us if I offered him a plate of waraq enab to-go as a thank you goodbye, if I had managed to make them. Instead, I say "thank you," and "see you in June." Time, between now and then, for me to stew the leaves.

Morocco

Chocolate
Cake

By **Mohamed Khalfouf**

Translated by
Mbarek Sryfi

I suddenly found myself, in addition to taking care of my mother, obliged to do the housework: sweeping, cleaning, washing clothes, cooking… I remember I was twelve years old when I first fried an egg; I let it cook for ten minutes, while watching TV, until it got totally burned. But now I can take care of myself with whatever is cheap and available: eggs, tuna, macaroni, rice, potatoes, lentils. And sometimes—always improvising, but somehow it works—I use vegetables to make a meal.

I wake up early, make a cup of coffee, and chug it down. I warm up the leftover potatoes, wake my mother, wash her face with a wet towel, feed her potato soup, or any sort of soup, wipe her mouth, and give her the medicine. I tuck her in and head to the university. On my way back home, I stop by the bakery to buy a loaf of bread, which at that time, around midday, is always warm and delicious. I also buy a can of tuna or a few eggs, and sometimes I buy a sandwich from one of the restaurants around Hay Atlas. I buy macaroni, eggs, and cans of tuna in bulk so I don't have to keep going back to the store.

In the evening, I make my mother potato soup: I chop potatoes and onions into a big pot that can hold a lot of soup, mashing the ingredients into a pulp. Sometimes, I mix different vegetables: carrots, zucchini, pumpkin, turnips. I write in the kitchen on the old wooden table, surrounded by utensils, spices, the fridge, the stove. I write a poem or a short story as I stir the pot or the frying pan. I return to my writing, then add oil or spices or salt to the mix, and sauce to the macaroni.

At first, I thought it would be hard to combine the strenuous housework with writing, which requires a lot of focus, but I have succeeded in marrying the two. I found out later that Sylvia Plath used to manage the housework, caring for her two children while writing, even when she was writing *The Bell Jar*. She wrote diligently, and also took care of her home. On Saturdays, I get a good night's sleep. I wake up fresh and in a good mood. I have breakfast, bring my mother to her seat, feed her, and give her the medicine; I chat a bit to break the silence, then leave the house around 10:30 to go shopping. I buy fish and vegetables, spices, salt and garlic and coffee, tomato paste, vinegar, and rice. I manage to handle the shopkeepers and money while also finding good and fresh ingredients. I stop by the bakery and buy a lot of bread, because the bakeries are closed on Sundays, and I keep it in plastic bags in the fridge. At home, I make myself a cup of coffee so I can focus while I cook. I take the vegetables out of the plastic, put them in the fridge, and wash what I need for lunch. I fill up the jars with spices, then salt, and then coffee. I wash the rice three times, then put it on to boil. I put potatoes in another pot. I take a sip of my coffee. I wash the fish in the sink and meticulously gut it, which leaves its slimy residue on my hands. I peel the onion, which makes me cry as usual, but I can bear onion tears.

I sip my coffee, now getting cold. I put the onion in the frying pan with a little bit of oil and I mix it; I drain the potatoes and add them to the onions, then add salt and spices and keep stirring so it doesn't burn. I dip the fish in spiced flour and heat the oil. From a distance, I put the fish in the hot oil, one fish at a time. And the street noise and the sounds of the TV reach me in the kitchen. I put rice on a plate, cut the cucumbers and tomatoes, add salt and vinegar. I put the spicy fried fish on another plate and leave the potatoes and onion in the frying pan. I'll have finished my cup of coffee. I carry all that to the dining room to have lunch and watch TV.
In a linen bag, my mother had put eight full-color cookbooks and four medium-sized notebooks. The notebooks were filled with recipes, even the margins, and depending on the size of the rectangular margins, she had fit an additional recipe or two—a plethora of recipes for dishes both sweet and salty, meats, chicken and fish dishes, sauces, creams, and pastas. The eight books had pictures of the dishes, and pictures of hands preparing the dishes, with well-elaborated recipes and detailed instructions. I remember my mother would spend a lot of her time reading these books and writing in them, especially in the afternoon, sitting at the same place where she was now lying motionless. The sunlight would stream in through the window, falling on her as she leafed through the pages. After that, she'd go to the kitchen and begin to make a cake. I used to watch her, curious, although mostly with a lack of interest, as she mixed the ingredients, made the creams, put them in the oven, and after a while she brought them out warm, or cold from the fridge, covered in cream or chocolate: delicious.

I never found out how my mother changed, after her return from Damascus, from a philosophy student into an in-demand pastry chef, making cakes for wedding parties, events, and funerals, sweets both traditional and modern, entrees, and birthday cakes with names and "Happy Birthday" drawn on them.
Cars stopped in front of our building to pick up their orders; they would call later to praise the cakes and thank the hands

that had crafted them, the hands I wash daily and which have grown stiff from lack of movement, the fingers becoming like tree roots.

I tried to understand the relationship between Plato, Aristotle, Ibn Hayan, Ibn Rushd, Spinoza, Heidegger, Sartre and eggs, yeast, cacao, Chantilly cream, and gelatin paper; maybe cooking was a philosophy, too.
Amidst all these various recipes, which seemed so difficult, full of ingredients and notes, requiring a lot of skill and precision, I stumbled upon a recipe for a chocolate cake. It was an easy recipe, with only a few ingredients and not much prep time. So, for the first time in my life, I decided to make a cake.

I wrote down the ingredients and returned the notebook to its linen bag. I gathered the ingredients: flour, eggs, yeast, oil, sugar, cacao, nuts, raisins, and half a bar of dark chocolate. I mixed the ingredients, adding the nuts, raisins, and chocolate, working all the ingredients together into a consistent dough, as it said in the recipe. I buttered the cake pan and sprinkled it with a bit of flour. Before that, I had to preheat the oven; all of this took some time. Carefully, I put the pan in the oven, like a mother dropping her child at daycare for the first time, and I kept watching the cake through the oven's glass panel as it swelled and rose and began to turn a dark brown.

As I was moving the cake from the pan to the plate, it broke in half: one half in my hand and the other stuck to the pan. Crumbs on the marble countertop, my hand burning with half the cake, and the other half deformed in the pan. I took a bite from the half in my hand; it was delicious, sweet and hot, raisins melted in chocolate. For a moment, I was filled with an overwhelming bliss. It was a success; I even saw the clear glitter of happiness in my mother's eyes. I had my first cake that evening with great delight.

At first, I hated cooking and thought of it only as a means to fill the belly. I also thought only a certain few could cook, mothers and chefs. But in time, I built an intimate relationship with the things in the kitchen: spoons, knives, forks, plates, cups, the frying pan, the pot, salt, spices, oil, vinegar, sugar, the stove, and other things that help my focus. I began to see the kitchen as a philosophy, exactly like the act of writing. Preparing a plate was like writing a text. Just as there are dozens of ways to prepare spaghetti, for example, there are dozens of ways to write a novel or short story. Cooking and writing: two quests for quality, precision, and flavor.

This chocolate cake was not the best cake in the whole world, but it was good enough, at least for me, because it had its own special taste. I am a writer who strives to bake good, delicious texts that have their own special tang.

Egypt

Rice Pudding for Two

By **Rehab Bassam**

Translated by
Fatima El-Kalay

For a bowl of rice pudding for two, you'll need:

A quarter cup of rice—but first take the milk out of the fridge.

Arrange the grains of rice on a big white plate; pick out any impurities.

Put everything aside—your bitterness, your grief, your anger, your disappointment, and any negative thoughts.

Prepare plenty of patience and spontaneous smiles. Take your time with the steps; never trust a recipe that claims you can rush the process.

For best results, make sure you are alone in the kitchen, or better still, the whole house. Shut off all mobile phones; slip into something comfortable.

Wash the rice more than once, until its water runs clear, then soak it in two cups of warm (not boiling) water for thirty minutes.

In the meantime, pour five cups of milk into a clear glass jug. Relax. With utmost tenderness, hold the jug between your palms, allowing your palms to hug it. This hug will warm up the milk. Think happy thoughts, hum a dreamy song:

I belong to my love, and my love belongs to me
hey, little white bird
no more sadness or reproach
I belong to my love, and my love belongs to me

Remember that all your steps will become part of the rice pudding, and that everyone who eats it will sense this. Even the song becomes part of it.

Especially the song.

In a medium-sized pot, pour the milk. Drain the rice and add it. Stir gently in one direction for fifteen minutes.

My love calls out to me
he says: winter has gone
the wood pigeon has returned
and the apple blossoms

Now think of a beautiful word, or a long kiss, or a warm smile across a crowded room, or a satisfying hug.

Hum, yes. And smile too.

Yes, yes. Let your eyes twinkle; it befits the rice pudding.

The morning's at my doorstep
and the dew
and in your eyes
my spring blossomed into beauty

Take a pinch of cinnamon with one hand and a pinch of vanilla with the other; delicately sprinkle both into the mixture. Now rub your hands together and bring your attention to your neck, patting your palms against it. This detail is essential for a good rice pudding.

On low heat, continue to stir the pudding for fifteen more minutes until the rice is tender. Whisper a secret close to the pot. Choose your secret wisely. Add half a cup of sugar and continue to stir, until dissolved, completely, completely. The sugar always comes last, after a long wait. The lower the heat, the sweeter the dish.

Sigh.

My love calls me
I come without question
to the one who stole sleep from me
and my peace of mind

Serve warm in a pink glass dish, topped with a sprinkling of cinnamon.

With partially opened lips, place your special imprint on its surface.

Eat slowly with your fingers, with someone you love.

I am on his path
his path is beauty
hey, lovers' sun
weave our story

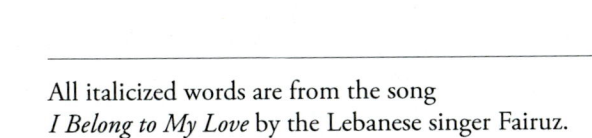

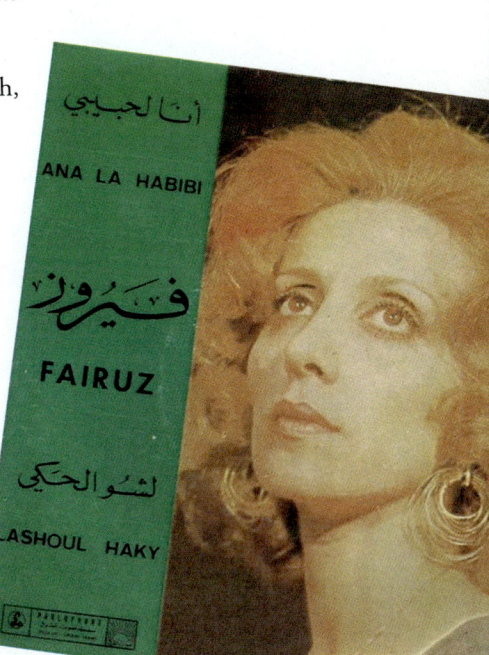

All italicized words are from the song
I Belong to My Love by the Lebanese singer Fairuz.

Read & Eat

Sandwiches Before the Earl
Muffaletta

By **Nawal Nasrallah**

A few years ago, I read a book on the global history of the sandwich by Bee Wilson. I was disappointed by the author's decision to dismiss the medieval Arab contribution as culturally irrelevant to the things we call a "sandwich" because the family of Middle Eastern wraps has, in Wilson's words, "a lineage which is entirely separate from the European sandwich; and they lack a single name to unify them." [1] Such unfortunate misconceptions are no doubt largely based on the assumption that the sandwich originated exclusively in Europe and that the English sandwich—two slices of loaf, enclosing some sort of filling—is its prototype. This assumption further suggests that the Middle Eastern sandwich-family is all about wraps. In fact, what we know today of medieval Arab cooks' practices in the art of making sandwiches, for which they had more than one category name, is undeniably significant and warrants it a place in any account of the evolution of the sandwich. If the Arab lineage were irrelevant to the European sandwich, then how could we account for a sandwich like the *muffaletta* of New Orleans, said to originate in Sicily, and whose name and composition have Arabic origins?

---

[1] Wilson, *Sandwich: A Global History* (Reaktion Books, 2010), pp. 29–30.

It is easier to ponder the troubles of the world with a richly stuffed muffaletta in hand.

The 4th Earl of Sundwich by Thomas Gainsborough

Here's how it all began:

Western history usually relegates the "official invention" of the sandwich to mid-eighteenth-century England, when John Montagu, the fourth Earl of Sandwich, started asking for his meals to be served between two layers of bread. John Montagu was an avid gambler, or perhaps a workaholic, who did not want lengthy table-dinners to interrupt whatever it was he was doing. Speculation goes that people took notice and imitated him, asking for whatever it was Sandwich had, and within a short time food served that way was given the name "sandwich."

As far as naming goes, the Montagu story is of course plausible, but Montagu was by no means the first to eat food this way. Consumption of sandwiches goes hand in hand with bread-making, which must have happened thousands of years back in human history. It was all about convenience.

All kinds of bread—flat and spongy, leavened and unleavened, large and small, malleable and cracker-like—were at the disposal of diners of the entire ancient Near East. In ancient Mesopotamia both the clay oven *tannur* and the brick oven *furn* were used in making more than 300 varieties of bread. From scenes depicted on ancient Egyptian temple walls, we can see that fillings were added between two layers of bread to resemble sandwiches, and cylindrical breads were made that looked like pinwheels. As for ancient Greece and Rome, they looked to the Near East for assistance and inspiration. In his "Life of Luxury," Sicilian-Greek gourmet Archestratus (fourth century BCE) recommended that, for the best results, Phoenician or Lydian bakers should be hired, as they knew how to make every kind of daily bread.

The first documented appearance of a sandwich goes back to nearly the beginning of our common era, when Rabbi Hillel the Elder (110 BCE–10 CE), sometimes referred to as Hillel the Babylonian, wrapped up the Passover sacrificial lamb and bitter herbs and ate them in fulfillment of one of the Biblical Passover rules, "they shall eat the flesh in that night, roast with fire, and unleavened bread; and with bitter herbs they shall eat it" (Exodus 12:8). What Hillel ate was by no means the first invented sandwich. People must have been consuming meat, herbs, and vegetables wrapped in flatbread, leavened or unleavened, for millennia before him. What he actually started was the first *korech*, also *karich*, a generic name for wrapping, which was the designation specifically for a wrap or rolled-up sandwich. **2** Apparently there were attempts to call this sandwich a "Hillelit" after the name of its "inventor," but the name never caught on.

After Hillel made his *korekh*, we had to wait several centuries for further documented evidence of the sandwich in the Near East. It next appeared during medieval Muslim rule. Extant records of the Arab sandwich comprise a variety of sources, ranging from recipes in cookbooks and books on dietetics and medicine to food-poems and anecdotes in contemporary chronicles and belle letters. More or less, the same types of bread that the ancients had at their disposal continued to be baked in the ovens of medieval Arabo-Muslim cooks, be they the clay oven tannur for the flatbread, the iron plate or marble slab for the thin sheets of ruqaq bread, or the brick oven furn, where spongy, crusty, and domed breads were produced. With these breads, a lot of sandwiches were made.

In al-Mas'udi's tenth-century *Muruj al-Dhahab*, a poem by the famous Abbasid poet of Baghdad Ibn al-Rumi (d. 896) describes how to construct a sandwich, which he calls *wast*, in which the stuffing is put between two layers of bread: **3**

A depiction of the royal bakery from an engraving in the tomb of Ramesses III in the Valley of the Kings. There are many types of loaves, including ones that are shaped like animals. 20th dynasty. WikiCommons

2 *There is a similar term in Arabic, which is karakha 'wrap,' 'encircle,' or 'roll' (see, for instance, Lisan al-'Arab, s.v. k-r-kh). Cf. the Persian term charkh, which designates 'wheel.'*

3 *See the Arabic poem in Muruj Al-Dhahab: accessed April 17, 2021. English translation of the poem is mine.*

> You, seeker of delicious food, take a couple of fine breads, round and thick,
> The likes of which no one has seen.
> Slice off the top crusts, so that you make them thin.
> Spread onto one: finely minced grilled chicken, delectable and delicate, which a mere puff would melt.
> On this, arrange lines of almond intersected with lines of walnut.
> Let its dots be cheese and olive, and its vowels mint and tarragon,
> Now take boiled eggs, and with their dirhams [egg white] and dinars [egg yolk] the *wast* adorn. **4**
> Give it a dusting of salt—but not much—just what it needs.
> Inspect it with your eyes for a second or two, for the eyes have a share in it, too.
> Look at it appreciatively until your eyes have their fill,
> Then cover it with the other bread and eat with joy.

In addition to the *wast* sandwiches (pl. *awsat*), other varieties were made. *Shatirat* (or *shata'ir*, sg. *shatira*) were analogous to what today are called open-faced sandwiches. Some were simply coated with olive oil and sharp cheese, and these were said to excite the appetite, while others were a bit more elaborately done. In the fourteenth-century *Kitab sifat al-at'ima*, **5** for instance, there is a version that is covered with a yogurt mix and infused with the smoke of walnut shells:

> To make *shatayir*, take fine-tasting yogurt, mix it with some of the fermented sauce *murri* **6** and thyme. Spread the mix on soft *ruqaq* bread and moisten it with extra virgin olive oil. Turn a sieve over it and create smoke by [burning] a piece of walnut [shell] and a drop of oil beneath it. Do this several times until the entire bread is redolent with the aromatic smoke. Roll the bread while it is hot and eat it, or keep it protected from the air [covered] until needed. (p. 37)

We also sample another *shatira* sandwich that goes all the way back to ninth-century Baghdad, as documented in al-Warraq's tenth-century Baghdadi cookbook *Kitab al-Tabikh*, which allocates chapter 23 to these foods. This *shatira* was made by no less than the Abbasid gourmet Prince Ibrahim b. al-Mahdi (d. 839), half-brother of Harun al-Rashid. The crusty edges and top of a brick-oven bread are sliced off, and the face is spread with a fermented condiment called *binn*, then slathered with walnut oil. It is then toasted on a grill set on a brazier, and after smearing it with the yolk of soft-cooked eggs, it is good to eat. Interestingly, Ibn al-Mahdi illustrated his recipe with a short poem, which today would be replaced with a foodporn photo:

> What a delicious sandwich on the brazier I made, slathered with *binn* and walnut oil!
> Fragrant and shining, as if the *binn* was embalmed with ambergris and musk.
> Of nigella seeds, I used what was needed; as for fennel, I did sprinkle some.
> Olive oil I made sure to add, for it gives a luscious coating and a saffron glow.
> Smeared with egg yolks, with cheese sprinkled, it's looking like speckled embroidered silk.
> As colorful as striped silk, it exudes musk and camphor.
> And the taste is rich as pure honey, for I used the best of aromatic spices. **7**

Also from al-Warraq's cookbook, we learn how to make the *bazmaward*, which is similar to today's rolled and wrapped sandwiches, sliced into pinwheels. One of the recipes, a Baghdadi style *bazmaward*, is unique in that it was baked in the *tannur* oven after rolling. Raw meat is pounded into a fine mince along with kidney fat, onion, fresh herbs, and rue, with a lot of spices. Then the meat is kneaded with five raw eggs,

4 Dirhams are silver coins, and dinars, gold ones.

5 This is an augmented version of thirteenth-century al-Baghdadi's Kitab al-Tabikh, MS 11 Sina'a Taymur in the National Library in Cairo. The MS I used is slightly different from Kitab Wasf al-At'ima al-Mu'tada, translated by Charles Perry in Medieval Arab Cookery (Prospect Books, 2001), pp. 275–465.

6 It is cereal-based; today's soy sauce may replace it in such recipes.

كتاب الطبيخ
ابن الوراق

Two pages from Kitab al-tabikh in the National Library of Finland

7 Al-Warraq, Kitab al-Tabikh, English translation, Nawal Nasrallah, Annals of the Caliphs' Kitchens (Brill, 2007), pp. 151–152.

along with a small amount of chopped garlic and onion. Sheep caul fat is spread on a malleable *ruqaq* bread, and the pounded meat mix is spread all over it. Five boiled eggs, shelled but left whole, are arranged in a row along the meat. The bread is tightly rolled up and trussed with a cleaned intestine, and then it's tied to four wooden sticks with a thread, lowered into the tannur, and placed on a flat tile that's directly on the fire. When the roll is done, it is sliced crosswise into pinwheels, which the recipe calls *bazmaward*. **8**

Equally interesting is the vegetarian version of *bazmaward* that fasting Christians could eat during Lent. It was called *ruhbani*, a name that derives from *rahib* or "monk," found in the fourteenth-century *Kitab sifat al-at'ima* mentioned above:

> A recipe for *bazmaward ruhbani*: Take *ruqaq* bread, which has been infused with aromatic smoke [e.g. of burning walnut shells with olive oil]. Spread it flat and moisten it with the hot liquid of *sikbaj* thickened with [crushed] almond. **9** Add just enough so that the bread does not disintegrate. Arrange a row of egg whites [boiled and sliced] in the middle, and spread the rest of the space with [chopped] tarragon and green olives. Roll it, slice it, and fill up a platter with it.

The significance of the Medieval Arab sandwich

The "inventory" of the extant medieval Arab sandwich recipes is impressively varied. As a cold dish, it was served before the main hot meal to facilitate digestion. It was a popular snack food, good for nibbling and passing around in large trays at social gatherings, similar to today's *hors d'oeuvres*. To obtain neatly cut slices, mess-free, cooks used a special knife, sharp and thin-bladed. It was called *sikkin al-bazmaward*.

The sandwich was an emblem of elegance and luxury. Among the nicknames heaped on it: *luqmat al-khalifa* (caliph's morsel), *narjis al-ma'ida* (narcissus of the table), and the luscious *fakhdh al-sitt* (lady's thigh). Dreaming of *bazmaward* was a good omen: it foretold enjoying a leisurely life with lots of easy money. In high society, social decorum dictated that *awsat* and *bazmaward* should be eaten sliced thinly. Eating whole rolls of *bazmaward* was not unheard of, although it was looked down upon as gluttony. An anecdote tells how a glutton once ordered his cooks to prepare *bazmaward*. He particularly asked for them to be left unsliced. He wanted them to be stuffed with chicken fat, clarified butter, herbs, eggs, cheese, olives, and walnuts. Soon enough a "pyramid" of the filled rolls was brought in a square tray, and one roll after the other, he devoured them all. **10**

During the Fatimid caliphate in Egypt, between the tenth and the twelfth centuries, sandwiches were conveniently offered in large trays to the public to celebrate the end of Ramadan, both to eat and to take home. As fast food, sandwiches were cheaply purchased from the cookshops in the food markets. From books on marketplace food inspection, we learn that some shops specialized in selling grilled meat thinly sliced (*musharrah*), and others sold *shawi mardud* (minced grilled-meat). While mincing and slicing, the cooks moistened the meat with the dripping fats and juices and soured it with sumac or lemon juice. We may safely assume that these grilled meats were conveniently stuffed or wrapped in bread and served like today's *shawarma* sandwiches.

Strangely enough, no written records of such sandwiches came down to us from the Ottoman era, ubiquitous as they had been before this time. This surely does not mean

---

8 Ibid, p. 149. Etymologically, the name may mean 'a tightly wrapped roll,' based on a possible combination of *warid* 'log,' and *bazm*, which designates rolling something tightly (Lisan al-'Arab, s.vv. w-r-d and b-z-m).

9 *Sikbaj* was stew soured with vinegar, usually cooked with beef but for Lent it was thickened and enriched with crushed nuts.

Fragment of a bowl, 11th century. Fatimid dynasty, found in Fustat, Egypt. Brooklyn Museum

10 al-Tabari, Tarikh al-rusul wa-l-muluk, p. 2129, online: http://www.alwaraq.net/Core/waraq/coverpage?bookid=49, accessed April 17, 2021.

that they didn't exist. An anonymous lithograph made in the 1850s portrays a typical seller of döner, which is grilled meat thinly shaved from layers of slices of meat threaded onto a vertically revolving spit. The picture also shows a pile of round and not-so-flat discs of bread, similar to the medieval brick-oven bread used in stuffing the *awsat* sandwiches. 11 The modern-day *shawarma* sandwich is a sure descendant of this tradition.

The appeal of sandwiches never faded, but their medieval names surely did. *Shata'ir* (the split) is now the "official" name of the sandwich in standard Arabic, while other names were coined in various dialects. In Iraq, for instance, it is *laffa* (roll, wrap) or *sandawich* that designates both wraps and stuffed hollowed-out brick-oven bread. In the Levant, *'arayis* sandwiches are none other than the *bazmaward* and *awsat* of medieval times. Pita bread is opened up, moistened with olive oil, filled, and then rolled and cut into smaller pieces; or else left flat and divided into sections. In *Armenian Food: Fact, Fiction, and Folklore*, we are assured that spreading filling on lavash bread and rolling it tightly was a popular fast food and a basic meal for many generations of Armenians.12 It was the Armenian immigrants in America who popularized lavash bread as well as the sandwiches made with it. The Armenian Hye and Aram sandwich was sold in delis as whole rolls or sliced into pinwheels, exactly like *bazmaward* was served in medieval times.

The Arab sandwich goes west

While the medieval east yielded an impressive repertoire of sandwiches, it is a different story when we turn west to al-Andalus and Sicily, where Arabs ruled for centuries. From the entire western region, only two Arabic cookbooks have survived, namely the anonymous thirteenth-century *Anwa' al-saydala fi alwan al-at'ima* and *Fidalat al-khiwan fi tayyibat al-ta'am wa-l-alwan* by scholar Ibn Razin al-Tujibi. Not a single mention is made in them of *awsat*, *bazmaward*, or *shata'ir*. This is rather puzzling, since food from the Mashreq was a significant inspiration in the development of Andalusi cuisine. The situation in Sicily is equally intriguing. In his book *Cucina Paradiso: The Heavenly Food of Sicily*, food writer Clifford Wright comments:

> When I asked Sicilians what the foundation was for *cucina arabo-sicula*, they nearly all gave the same answer – folklore and intuition. One has to look at what the Arabs brought to Sicily in the way of new crops and recognize what the Arabs themselves ate.

Folklore has indeed preserved two Arab dishes, which were said to have been named after the eleventh-century Arab Emir of Catania, Muhammad ibn al-Thumna (d. 1062), who appealed to Norman troops from southern Italy to help him defeat his Muslim adversaries on the island around 1053. This opened the door for the Normans to take control of the island. One might speculate whether that was how the beloved Arab recipes of this Muslim leader survived the hostilities and persecution his Muslim brethren endured in the centuries to come.

The dish that concerns us here is a chicken sandwich, named *Pasticcio di Mohammed ibn Itmnah* (al-Thumna). As described in J. C. Grasso, *The Best of Southern Italian Cooking*, round and crusty bread is cut in half horizontally and hollowed out. The stuffing is made of a combination of finely chopped cooked chicken, almonds, pista-

---

11 Interestingly, what is now called shawarma in the Middle East is the Arabized form of the old Ottoman Çevirme, which in modern Turkish is replaced with döner. Both mean 'meat cooked while revolving.'

Döner in Turkey;
Taken by James Robertson in 1855, this is considered to be the first döner photo.

12 Irina Petrosian & David Underwood, Armenian Food (Yerkir Publishing, 2006), p. 30. Lavash is beyond doubt no other than the ruqaq bread used in making the Arab medieval bazmaward sandwiches. In fact, in the Armenian vernacular this thin bread was called parag-hatz, where parag is the corrupted form of the Arabic waraq (paper, leaf), used in medieval times to designate the thin sheets of ruqaq bread.

chios, capers, eggs, and the crumbled hollowed-out breadcrumbs, all moistened with the chicken broth. The upper crust of the bread is put back and the bread is returned to the oven to slightly crisp. The sandwich is served at room temperature sliced, as we may reasonably assume was usually done with medieval *awsat*. In Sicily, it is deemed a typical example of the Arabo-Sicilian kitchen. And justifiably so. As it happens, a similar recipe survives from the Arab east that is clearly akin to Ibn Thumna's sandwich. It was called *awsat Misriyya* (Egyptian sandwich) and is documented in the cookbook *al-Wusla ila l-habib fi wasf al-tayyibat wa-l-tib* by Aleppan historian Ibn al-'Adim (d. 1262). **13**

13 *The Arabic recipe and the English translation can be found in Charles Perry, Scents and Flavors (NY University Press, 2017), pp 72–5.*

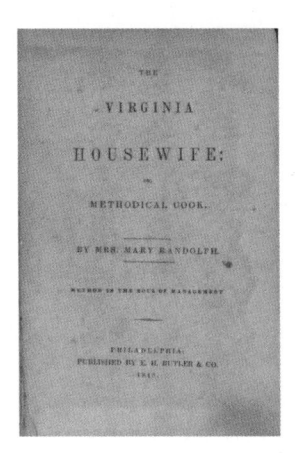

Eventually, Ibn al-Thumna's sandwich found its way to the New World, where a similar sandwich is included in a nineteenth-century American cookbook; however, it uses oysters for the filling instead of chicken. The book is *The Virginia House-Wife* by Mary Randolph, the first truly American cookbook, published in 1829. It includes recipes from southern cooking, England, France, and Spain, among other places, and it is highly likely that Sicilians introduced this sandwich to America. They were the first mass wave of immigrants to Port of New Orleans, and it is in New Orleans that we find the last piece, so to speak, to our puzzle. The significance of this sandwich is that it has been recognized as an earlier variant on a New Orleans sandwich called po'boy, first traced in America in 1875, popularized by Sicilian immigrants. Now, closely related to the po'boy and even more interesting, because of its name, is another New Orleans sandwich called the *muffaletta*.

The Virginia Houswife, edition of 1848

The origin of *muffaletta* is unanimously acknowledged as Sicilian. It is a large and round sesame-encrusted bread that is hollowed out and filled with thin layers of Italian cold cuts of meat, cheese, and a chopped-olive salad mainly composed of olives, pickled vegetables, and herbs, along with lemon juice and olive oil. It is dressed with extra olive oil and sour juices to moisten the bread and these give the sandwich its distinctive flavor and texture.

The "official" date of the sandwich's birth is usually said to be 1906, when the Sicilian immigrant Salvatore Lupo "created" it as a po'boy sandwich. "Created" might be a bit of a stretch. Lupo was a Sicilian immigrant, and in his homeland the popular *muffaletta* bread, eaten sometimes stuffed with meat and other things, was an ordinary meal all over Sicily for many generations. What he did was give the sandwich a name by calling it after the bread used in making it, the *mafalada* (variants: *muffolette, muffuletta, mafalda*). Where did this name come from? Nobody knows exactly. In Western sources, it is said to be connected to the Old French *moufflet*, which means "soft," used to describe bread. Some speculate that it is Sicilian for "hollow bread."

I believe that our key to this puzzle lies in its Sicilian Arabic roots. More than a millennium ago, the Arabs ruled Sicily, and Arabic for some time was the island's official language. Today in Sicily, many foods still carry Arabic names, albeit with an Italian ring. In the case of the bread *muffaletta*, the Arab roots are sometimes acknowledged, but no one has yet made the linguistic connection.

Two men eating poboy sandwiches in New Orleans, Louisiana in the 1930s; State Library of Louisiana

Bread varieties similar to *muffaletta*—round, oven-baked, thickish, crusty, and spongy—were known all over the medieval Islamic world. It was the bread used in making *awsat*. Apparently, bread twisted in this form acquired the name *mafalada* in Muslim Sicily. The word was derived from the Arabic *malfut* or *maflut*, which in this context means "wound," "coiled," "wrapped," "rolled up," or "twisted." Although this common bread is shaped in a variety of ways, it is the serpentine twisted form, the *mufallata*, that is deemed the most orthodox.

In commenting on the ridiculously extreme turns some American cooks have taken in constructing the sandwich, such as the mishmash Dagwood or the unwieldy Scooby-Doo, Bee Wilson remarks that, by contrast:

> There are such things as the *Muffaletta*, that delicious New Orleans specialty in which layers of piquant olive salad and cold meat are placed inside an entire hollowed-out loaf, or the oyster loaf, where cooked oysters similarly fill out a hollow roll. There is a certain integrity to these sandwiches. [14]

Thus, our author unwittingly gives credit where it's due. This "certain integrity" stems from the weight of centuries worth of history and tradition behind the sandwich, which evolved in the medieval Arab world. Medieval Arab cooks played a considerable role in the evolution of sandwiches through the myriad varieties they hospitably passed around to guests or sold as fast food at the grillers' cookshops in food markets. The cultural and lineal bearings they had on the metamorphoses of the modern sandwich cannot be denied. Their creativity is apparent in both the form and content of the sandwiches; recognizing their contributions will give them a well-deserved place at the table.

> **A medieval recipe** for the pinwheel sandwiches, *bazmaward*, from tenth-century *Kitab al-Tabikh* by Ibn Sayyar al-Warraq (chapter 23). [15] It was made for the Abbasid Caliph al-Mutawakkil (d. 861):

Use cold [cooked] meat of two legs and shoulders of a kid or lamb. Finely shred the meat into thread-like pieces. Choose whatever you like of leaf vegetables, excluding watercress (*jirjir*) and endives (*hindiba*). Finely chop them until they resemble sesame seeds and mix [part of] them with the shredded meat. Set the mixture aside.

Now choose good quality sharp cheese, scrape it with a knife, and collect the scraped cheese. Coarsely grind walnuts and add them [with the cheese] to the [set-aside meatless] chopped vegetables. Also add some chopped herbs and rue. A portion of the chopped vegetables should have been set aside unmixed with the meat. Next, peel and chop some olives and add them to the [meatless] chopped vegetable mixture.

Spread a soft and large *ruqaqa* [similar to lavash bread], cover it with some of the meatless vegetable mixture and sprinkle it with seasoned salt. Next, spread the meat and vegetable mixture [to which you should have added] some spices. Then arrange a layer of eggs sliced lengthwise. Next, spread another layer of the meat and vegetable mixture followed by a layer of the meatless vegetable mixture. Sprinkle them with fine-tasting salt and drizzle them with sweet vinegar and rose water.

Tightly roll the bread with the filling and slice it crosswise into discs. Arrange the [pinwheels] on a platter and pass them around, God willing.

An earlier version of this essay appeared in *Traveling through Time*, published by the Finnish Oriental Society, 2013.

[14] Wilson, p. 88.

[15] English translation by Nawal Nasrallah, Annals of the Caliphs' Kitchens (Brill, 2007), p. 150.

*Muffaletta bread in its original serpentine shape before and after baking and Bazmaward sandwiches.
Photos: Nawal Nasrallah*

Contributors

Asmaa Abdallah is a US-based literary critic and editor. She reviews Arabic fiction and interviews Arab authors for English-language publications such as *ArabLit*, *Mada Masr* and *Jadaliyya*. She also writes reader reports for publishers interested in Arabic translations. She studied literature for seven years, culminating in an MA in English and Comparative Literature from the American University in Cairo.

Moza Almatrooshi is a UAE-based conceptual artist & writer. She obtained an MFA from the Slade School of Fine Art in London in 2019. Almatrooshi's practice operates within the study of erased mythology of the Arabian Peninsula, and correlates these myths with the structures that are upheld by the present regional political climate. Through a fictive lens, her themes materialise in performances, moving image, audio media, as well as text. Moza's work has been performed in the Victoria & Albert Museum in London, selected by the ICA London and BBC for the New Creatives project, and displayed in the second Lahore Biennale.

Rehab Bassam is a lover of books and baked goods and is obsessed with cats. She studied English literature, worked in market research, advertising, editing, and translation. Spent almost ten delightful years working in publishing as an editor, translator, and publishing manager, with a passion for children's books. Currently living in Newcastle upon Tyne, UK, where she's raising two kids, runs an Arabic school, and is working on her first novel, and (maybe) a couple of children's books. Rehab was among the first Egyptian bloggers and one of the few who used her blog to publish her short stories. Selections of her blog posts were compiled in a book called *Rice Pudding for Two* (Dar El Shorouk, 2008), which became an instant bestseller.

Mariam Boctor is a writer, translator, researcher, and curator based in Egypt. Their work has been featured in *The Outpost*, *Mada Masr*, and the Contemporary Image Collective's publications *Taste of Letters*, and the forthcoming *Our Bodies Breathe underwater*. They are passionate about medicine, herbs, food, and the body. They love cats and sing sometimes.

Elissa Dallimore is an undergraduate student studying Arabic Studies and English Language and Literature at the University of Maryland, College Park. This is her first published translation, and she is indebted to Dr. Anny Gaul for helping her with this piece.

Fatima El-Kalay was born in England to Egyptian parents, but grew up in Scotland. She has a Master's degree in creative writing and writes poetry, short fiction, and creative nonfiction. Her work has been published in *Passionfruit*, *Rowayat*, *Anomalous Press* and *Poetry Birmingham Literary Review*. She was shortlisted for the London Independent Story Prize (LISP), and in *ArabLit Quarterly* for their first short story in translation competition. Fatima teaches fiction and poetry writing. She has a poetry book in progress and a collaborative short story collection that is due for publication. She is based in Cairo.

Samaa Elturkey is an independent researcher in sexuality. She loves cooking, animals, and writing and is always curious, especially about sexuality and body agency and autonomy.

Hacı Osman Gündüz (Ozzy) is a PhD candidate at Harvard University's Department of Near Eastern Languages and Civilization (NELC). His dissertation research focuses on Arabic literature of 16th-century Bilad al-Sham. His main interest is the literary milieu of Damascus during the first century of Ottoman rule (1516-1600). He also teaches classical Arabic at Harvard Divinity School's Summer Language Program (SLP).

Rania Helal is an Egyptian writer and freelance journalist. She has published several books and won many awards, including the Sawiris Award for her first published short story collection, دوار البر, and the Arab Fund for Arts and Culture award. Much of her work focuses on women's rights and issues.

Rym Jalil is a writer and poet based in Cairo. She wrote her first poem at the age of nine. Her first published poem, "Higher Power," was a collaboration with Sara Fakhry Ismail, which was released as part of a series of events on independent publishing at Cairo

Image Collective in September 2020. Most recently, she worked alongside other artists and writers eventually leading to a collective online publication *Our Bodies Breathe Underwater*, which featured three of her poems. In her poetry, mostly written in Egyptian dialect, she uses autobiographical events and abstract imagery interchangeably. Jalil holds a BA in Radio and TV broadcasting from Ain Shams University.

K

Donia Kamal is an Egyptian novelist and TV producer. She has written three novels: *Two Tales: She and Doha* (2009), *Cigarette Number Seven* (2012) which was translated into English by Nariman Youssef, and *Random Arrangements* (2019). She has also produced more than fifty documentary films and numerous television shows for various Arab networks. She currently lives between Egypt and the UAE.

Eman Abdelhamid Kamal majored in pharmacy, then pursued an old passion for arts through liberal arts and counseling psychology post-grad studies. She has been writing and blogging since 2009 at emanabdelhameed.blogspot.com. She loves coffee—no added sugar—jazz music, the smell of old books, and walking aimlessly.

Sohila Khaled is an Egyptian children's book illustrator and a comic artist. After graduating from the School of Pharmacy, she followed her passion for art and illustration. She participated in many exhibitions such as the Sharjah Exhibition for Children's Book Illustration 2019. She has illustrated many children's books for many Egyptian and Arabic publishers.

Mohamed Khalfouf is a Moroccan writer who was born in 1997 in Khouribga. He graduated from the Faculty of Arts, Division of Arabic Language in Fez. He has published stories and poems in many cultural newspapers, both Arab and international. His texts have been translated into many living languages, among them Hebrew, German, Georgian, Belarusian, and more. He has published a novel, *Zaman al-Hulm*, and a collection of stories, *Iqama fi l-qalaq*.

M

Mahitab Mahmoud is an Egyptian writer, translator, editor, and researcher living in the US. She holds a Master's Degree in Language Studies, a Specialized Translation Diploma, and a Bachelor of Arts Degree in Translation and Linguistics.

Amira Mousa is an independent journalist and the author of *Within the Household Orbit*. She has contributed to several anthologies, including a work of film criticism and *The Taste of Letters*. Amira is interested in digging more deeply into political and economic reflections on societies, places, and people, particularly in connection to questions of identity, by using the tools of ethnography and through investigating patterns.

N

Nawal Nasrallah is an independent scholar, previously professor of English at the universities of Baghdad and Mosul. She has published books and articles on the history and culture of Middle-Eastern and Arab food, including *Delights from the Garden of Eden* (Authorhouse 3003, Equinox 2013), *Dates: A Global History* (Reaktion Books 2011), and English translations of medieval Arabic cookbooks, *Annals of the Caliphs' Kitchens* (Brill 2007), *Treasure Trove of Benefits and Varieties at the Table* (Brill 2017), and forthcoming *Best of Delectable Foods and Dishes*, by Andalusi scholar Ibn Razin al-Tujibi.

R

Leonie Rau is *ArabLit*'s Editorial Assistant. She is currently studying for a master's degree in Islamic and Middle Eastern Studies at the University of Tübingen, Germany, and hopes to pursue a PhD after her graduation. She is a passionate home cook, but would love to spend more time reading rather than cleaning the kitchen.

S

Salma Serry is a food studies researcher, writer, and filmmaker, holding an MA in journalism from the American University of Cairo. She is currently pursuing a graduate degree in food studies at Boston University. Her current research focuses on cookbooks of 20th century Egypt, as well as issues of identity and citizenship in the United Arab Emirates through food. This year, Salma is exhibiting her work in Dubai and Jeddah, supported by Art Jameel. Her daily journeys on food and research are on @sufra_kitchen, an Instagram platform that invites followers to insights of food culture and history in SWANA.

Yasmine Shamma is a Lecturer of Modern and Contemporary Literature at the University of Reading, UK. She is the author of *Spatial Poetics: Second Generation New York School Poetry* (OUP, 2018), and the editor of *Joe Brainard's Art* (EUP 2019), *We Are the New York School* (EUP, 2022), and *Making Home Away* (forthcoming). She has been awarded a Leverhulme Research Fellowship for her book-length study on ways of talking about home in displacement.

Mbarek Sryfi, a poet and translator, teaches at the University of Pennsylvania. His work has been widely published in many journals and magazines, and anthologies including *Al-Arabiyya, Banipal, CEELAN Review, Metamorphoses, Middle Eastern Literatures, The Journal of North African Studies, Translation Review*, and *World Literature Today*. Sryfi has co-authored *Perspectives: Arabic Language and Culture in Film* (Alucen Learning, 2009), co-translated four books, *The Monarch of the Square* (Syracuse University Press, 2014), *The Arabs and the Art of Storytelling* (Syracuse University Press, 2014), *The Elusive Fox* (Syracuse University Press, 2016), *The Blueness of the Evening* (Arkansas University Press, 2018), and published a chapbook, *The Trace of a Smile* (Moonstone Press, 2018), which shared first place, and *City Poems-A Selection of poems* (Éditions L'Harmattan, 2020).

Zaina Ujayli recently graduated with an MA in English from the University of Virginia, where she studied twentieth century Arab diaspora women writers in the Americas. She is an incoming PhD student in American Studies & Ethnicity at the University of Southern California. Her articles have previously been published in *The New Arab* and *InkStick Media*.

Made in the USA
Las Vegas, NV
20 June 2021